Virga Tears

Virga Tears

*The True Story
of a Soldier's Sojourn
back to Vietnam*

by James H. Fallon

**Dickens Press
Irvine, California**

Copyright © 2001 by James Fallon

Published by Dickens Press, P.O. Box, Irvine, California 92616. 800-230-8158. All rights reserved. No part of this book may be used or reproduced by any means, electronic, mechanical, photocopying, recording, or other, without written permission from the publisher except in the case of brief quotations for use in articles and reviews.

Library of Congress Cataloging-in-Publication Data

Fallon, James H., 1947-
   Virga tears : the true story of a soldier's sojourn back to Vietnam / by James H. Fallon.
      p. cm.
   ISBN 1-880741-49-0 (pbk. : alk. paper)
   1. Vietnamese Conflict, 1961-1975--United States. 2. Vietnamese Conflict, 1961-1975--Veterans--United States. 3. Vietnamese Conflict, 1961-1975--Personal narratives, American. 4. Vietnamese Conflict, 1961-1975--Vietnam--Gia Nghäia. 5. Vietnamese Conflict, 1961-1975--Conscientious objectors--United States. 6. Fallon, James H., 1947-   .   I. Title.
   DS558 .F33 2001
   959.704'3'0922--dc21
                                                                    2001003319

Distributed to the trade by Dickens Press
ISBN 1-880741-49-0

Cover art copyright © 2001 by Jim Fallon.
Cover and interior design © 2001 by Michele Lanci-Altomare
All rights reserved.

To The Silent Soldier

PREFACE

There have been many stories and movies written about the Vietnam War. We've all been told of the covert policies and catastrophic actions taken by the U.S. Government during the only war we ever lost, and we've all lived through the tragic stories of the reluctant men who were drafted into the Armed Forces to engage in battles they didn't believe in.

Some of us, like myself, were adamantly opposed to America's role in the war and had the good fortune to be able to hide out in colleges and universities during the conflict. Like other opponents of the war, I had secretly savored the fact that I had always been right in my criticism of those who supported the war effort. I had taken the highest moral ground against the one war that the "heart of America" had never been able to resolve.

I had no idea that thirty years later my own attitudes and feelings about the war would be so thoroughly turned upside-down.

Following a rather casual comment I made in the winter of 1995, I would commit to taking a trip to one place I had no particular desire to visit—Vietnam. The country and culture just didn't intrigue me.

What made this venture more unlikely is that I would go with a person I had little in common with, and whose personality, tastes, background and political views were completely opposite to my own.

Nick and I were brought together by that most tenuous of family linkages one could imagine—we are brothers-in-law.

Swept off to Asia before I took even a moment to reflect on the choice of our first vacation together, we were visiting a place from Nick's past, a place he never spoke to anyone about, a place where he experienced things that he chose to keep deep inside for three decades.

It was, above all, a place he believed America should have been in 1967. After all, he was a West Point soldier who really believed in the war.

I never intended to write a story about our trip or the Vietnam War. But something happened to us during one day of our trip that rocked me deeply.

This story is about that one day in April 1996, a day we spent together in a small village in the Central Highlands of Vietnam where Nick had been stationed during the war.

I wrote this story for Nick and his family and for all the soldiers like Nick who fought and believed in the war, but who returned, abandoned, to suffer in silence for all these years. ～

Virga Tears

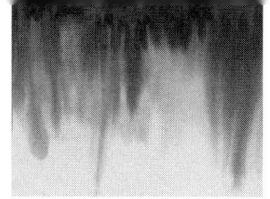

A Fair Enough Deal

IT SEEMED LIKE A FAIR ENOUGH DEAL. He could have his afternoon drive to the Highlands and I'd have the next afternoon at the racetrack. After all, in Nick's circles, a notch is cut in your belt for each officially registered, dangerous mountain you climb. In my social group, the more exotic racetracks you'd visit in your life, the loftier your stature. And the Saigon racetrack was a pretty juicy prize, considering the bitter pill the communist government must have swallowed when they were pressed hard to reopen this symbol of colonialism, capitalism and, vice. But before we could spend our last Sunday in Vietnam, we really needed to try to catch a ride to the Central Highlands. You see, in spite of the fact that Nick had climbed Kilimanjaro, Whitney, Rainier, and the Matterhorn, I knew he had one last mountain to climb, and we only had one Saturday left for him to make that final ascent.

A few months earlier I had intercepted a communiqué to my wife from Nick's wife—her sister. After 25 breathtakingly successful years on Wall Street,

Nick had called it quits as an investment banker. His retirement was long overdue and he had accumulated more wealth, respect, and friends in very high places than any man could ever want. He had everything, but he needed to let his hair down a bit. He'd been threatening to retire for a decade and when he finally did, I got the phone call. I think he'd always been a little jealous of my trips around the Third World. While he was dancing with the Duke's wife at the Vienna Winter Ball, I was navigating the gutters in some downright funky haunts in Africa and Asia. And now he wanted a piece of it.

I had been hearing some interesting stories from a Vietnamese colleague of mine at the university who had family and political contacts in his former homeland. He wanted me to explore some business opportunities with him in Vietnam. I mentioned this in passing to Nick, and, before I had a chance to give it a second thought, he was on a plane from New York to California to meet my colleague and firm up the plans for trip. The plans called for a three-week vacation in South China, Vietnam and Indonesia. It was to be a sort of business-culture-drinking-arm-punching-speedball tear for two 50+ year olds who still had just enough liver to crank out a trip a 25 year old would admire. The thing is, this trip had nothing to do with any of that. We never talked about it, but we both knew it.

Both of our wives and friends—but especially Nick's—were convinced the trip was a disaster waiting to happen. Everything about us is absolutely different. Nick is the introverted type who keeps all sphincters tight and well-controlled. I'm the extroverted type with a motor mouth and admirable bowel habits. No sphincter problems here. But the differences are worse than that. Much worse. I had fiercely objected to, and conveniently avoided, a war that Nick really believed in.

1967 was a good year for me. Safely tucked away at a small college in Vermont, I focused on books, Bacardi, and blasting the war. Mostly I was marching for more beer and broads on campus. In the summer of 1967, my wife-to-be and I had great fun making out and playing house with her nephew, Nick's first son, while her sister stared endlessly out the window in the way a bullfighter's wife stares when he is away fighting el toro. Meanwhile, a universe away, Nick was putting to good use his West Point education, ranger training, airborne training, intelligence training, and other hyper-tense pastimes in the Central Highlands of Dac Lac Province in Vietnam. He was stationed at the veritable cloaca of the Ho Chi Minh Trail, only a decent three iron shot from the Cambodian border, and he was alone—well, almost alone. He was there to train Rhade tribesmen of Montagnard fame, to intercept and destroy cadres of supply units down the trail to the deeper bowels of the Viet Cong war effort near Saigon.

I've already told you twice as much as what I knew about Nick's 1967 vacation in Vietnam. I had asked him many questions about the war after he returned in 1968 at the onset of the Tet offensive that changed the war and the groin of America. But Nick never told me fact one about his experiences—nothing. It was if every breathing moment of his life there was completely off-limits. So, like many of us upper middle class, educated white guys who never really knew too many friends who were actually in the war, I learned most of what that war was about from upper middle class, educated, white guys who made movies about the war they, too, had fortunately evaded. And it was neatly put away in my psyche as the War-I-Was-Absolutely-Right-About-Being-Against. What's more, Nick's thirty year silence and solitary emotional confinement only bolstered my ego and confident resolve that, like the other 20 percent of Americans at the time, I owned all the moral capital of that American Tragedy. Meanwhile, poor Nick, and all the other five hundred thousand soldiers who returned in one or more pieces from that party, had been sorely wrong about, or unlucky in, the war. From my point of view, this was probably a final opportunity for Nick to play the song over slowly, at 16⅙ rpm, just one last time. I was happy to play court jester on this return salvo of the soul to Dac Lac Province even if it meant we had to endure another absurd chapter of our odd couple game. Besides, I really wanted to bet the ponies the next day at the Saigon racetrack.

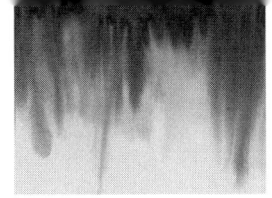

It Costs HOW Much?

NICK AND I WERE RUNNING OUT OF TIME. We flew into Saigon from Da Nang on Friday. And we had to fly out of Saigon on Sunday. Forget taking a later flight. When it's time to enter or leave Vietnam, you better hit the day on the button or you've got a high colonic full of bureaucratic bullshit on your hands. Then you can throw another thousand bucks in for breaking up the sacred flight schedule. Furthermore, we were not a couple of backpacking, limbic college dudes who thought it was really neat to screw up our schedule. Sure, Nick was retired and I was a tenured college professor with a purely artificial sense of time and work. But someone back home might find out we weren't in Complete Control of Everything, and then we'd lose face as 50 year old self-proclaimed cool guys.

This all meant that any jaunt to Dac Lac absolutely had to start, and end, on Saturday. I had carefully figured out the mileage—300 miles round trip—three hours up and three hours back, plus two hours for lunch and whatever else we were going to do up there. Hell, I was confident we could make it back to Saigon by dusk to do some degenerate honky-tonking in the fabled city of angst, until we collapsed in a heap.

The only problem was, how to get up there? My Vietnamese colleague in California had family in Saigon so I could try to coerce his brother, under the implied threat of a family disgrace if he couldn't deliver, to give us a ride. Or we could get the hotel concierge to arrange transportation for us. Or we could really get romantic and hire a helicopter to whisk us there in style. After all, I was going upstream with the real Colonel Kurtz and a chopper ride over the treetops, with Wagner blaring in my mind, would have been the perfect fantasy for me. The helicopter option turned out to be a little too romantic, at about two thousand dollars and no guarantee of a life hereafter. That left us about two hours to deal with my friend's brother or the concierge. The concierge at the Five Star Continental found someone almost willing to drive us there by Land Rover for about a dollar a mile, which was outrageous. We decided to take a chance, blow off the concierge, and wait for a return call from my friend's brother. He said that although two hours was not really enough time to set up a trip to nowhere the next morning, I was his brother's friend and he would do anything to help me. Okay, perhaps we should have opted for the helicopter.

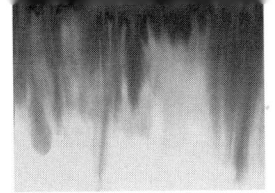

Did You Have a Restful Sleep, Dear?

The wake-up call arrived at 4:20 a.m., a tad too early for Nick. He got up slowly, purposefully, like he did on every morning of our trip. In fact he had the same look on his face as everyone does when they sleep in the same room with me. This includes my poor wife, who is known to my friends as "his poor wife." You see, I possess a talent—call it a gift—for making big music at night. And no human or animal, save for myself, has been able to make it through the long night without being rattled. Clinically, it has been awarded the only poetic description I know of in medicine—"heroic snoring."

As Nick shuffled to the toilet, I bounded up, refreshed and well-rested, and greeted him as I did every morning, "Did you have a restful sleep, dear?"

As others who have gone before him, Nick did not respond or look at me at all. I knew it would take him a good hour before he could regenerate enough good will to respond to me. I knew he was starting to seriously regret another deal the two of us had made at the beginning of the trip. He had been well-briefed on the racket I make when I slept, and he has a certain taste for top-end hotels that, well, I just couldn't handle those kind of tariffs. So instead of sleeping in separate rooms in more modestly priced accommodations, Nick and I agreed to sleep in the same room and split the five star rate. The deal was starting to wear on him.

He finally asked, "Are you okay?"

Of course, I was okay. I felt great. One friend said my snoring sounded like a tractor climbing a hill of corn flakes. But it was made worse when I was particularly fat, exhausted, or had smoked heavily the night before. Unfortunately for Nick, I was peaking out on all of those pathologies on this trip. To make matters worse, Nick and I would argue each night about everything under the sun and moon. And we both drank liberally during these heated exchanges. It helped limit the vitriol of the discussion and afforded Nick a way of getting into a stupor so he might fall asleep before I did. This never worked. Liquored up, I fall asleep even faster and deeper. And then the snoring is worse than anyone could possibly imagine. Under such circumstances, I have been known to keep entire hotels and condo complexes up all night. One time in 1985, a traveling companion, from whom I got separated at the Berlin wall, actually located my room in Prague by following the roar of my snoring from his balcony. And when I walked down to the lobby, the staff at the main desk, the concierge, the bellman, and the other guests all gave me that same derisive glare. But Nick never complained a bit about my snoring. He was known as a tough boss, stern father and husband. To those closest to him, he could be critical and demanding. But on this trip, he was definitely the most tolerant person I'd ever slept with.

I don't want to give the impression that Nick was the Quiet Man. While I was making noises at night, he was making noises during the day. From what I can tell, Nick has the same mild, charming touch of an affect that resembles Tourette's Syndrome that a surprising number of my colleagues have. Not the socially shocking form of Tourette's, replete with f-words and jerky twitches. His is more subtle. He'll give a hearty nasal snort, as if he's trying to clear a marble stuck in the deep recesses of his nose. This is followed by a rhythmic pattern of "HMM... HMM-HMM-HMM." He does this loud enough in public to make heads snap. For the first couple of days I'd answer "Yeah, Nick, what did you say?" until I realized he was completely unaware of the noises he was making, or he was unable to inhibit the noises, in Tourette's-like fashion. It's caused by a turned-up dopamine system in the brain. Too much dopamine is no picnic. Seriously unbalanced dopamine can cause schizophrenia, attention deficit disorder, and downright dangerous thrill-seeking behavior. So a little weird humming and nasal grunts are certainly at the low end of a jazzed-up dopamine spectrum. And considering that Nick is otherwise always in complete control and has absolutely no other bad habits or behavior, it's almost charming to hear him making those noises he can't control.

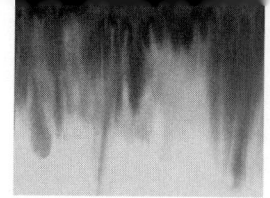

Your Coach Has Arrived, Sir

It was 5:30 a.m. and Nick had finished his first morning "HMMS." He flushed the toilet.

"You know, Jim, I told you we really don't have to go to the Highlands. There's plenty to do right here in the city," he offered unconvincingly.

I continued to pump sunshine for the yet-to-materialize ride to Dac Lac. "I'm sure our man has come up with a ride for us, or he's got his brother to answer to back home." At 5:45 the call came in, and all systems were go. "Show time, Nick," I boomed, "We've got a car, an experienced driver, and an interpreter—and only a hundred bucks for the whole day!"

Nick snorted and turned the hair dryer on. Even the twenty or so hairs on his head needed to be brought under control.

I took the opportunity to walk out on the balcony and fire up the very important first cigarette of the day. I always tried as hard as I could to get away from Nick when I lit up. He hated cigarettes—his father died at a relatively young age with emphysema from the little bastards—and

I knew he thought a little less of me for picking up this ridiculous habit again. An asthmatic medical school professor who still smokes? Nick didn't understand the Big Hook of smoking. My own dopamine system is easily swayed by such substances, and nicotine is an effective way to break up the boredom between meals. I had been successful in my college years through the 60's avoiding the really scary stuff. Like every other kid, I was surrounded by degenerates-in-training who were not satisfied with simply smoking bales of grass every day. That was not nearly enough of a buzz for them. Some of my roommates and friends went through enough LSD, mushrooms, Quaaludes, speedballs and handfuls of any and all pills to stop an elephant. I even found them sitting in the middle of our room one night snorting a baggie full of my camphorated opium rectal ointment. Involatile as that stuff was, they still managed to blow their minds with it. Don't get me wrong. I have no ethical problems with drugs. I inherited a taste for booze and the ponies from my father, who had great control with both. Besides, I had developed panic attacks rather suddenly at 18 years old and believe me, when your heart rate races to 120 and your blood pressure spikes to 240/140 for no apparent reason, you're not likely to press your luck on some hallucinogens or speed. Those attacks kept me far away from drugs. And allergic asthma kept me out of the Vietnam War. I learned never to curse my annoying, but life-saving miseries anymore.

Nick had no such luck. Disgustingly healthy, he still has an iron man's cardiovascular system and a baby face. Only a spot of baldness spoils his good looks. And I didn't let him forget that shiny spot.

"Get yer ass in gear, Nick. That hair dryer is not going to help your problem. Just wear the hat and no one will notice how old or bald you really are." "SNORT-HMM. HMM-HMM-HMM" was all I heard from the bathroom, as the hair dryer whirred to a stop. I then stepped back into our room, letting a cloud of cigarette smoke and hot, muggy Saigon air fill our suite. Nick did not complain.

Shitted, shaved and showered, we left the coolness and safety of our room. We walked out of the Continental Hotel and looked around with guarded optimism for our ride. The concierge was at the curb, talking to two gentlemen standing next to a mid 1980's white Toyota.

"Your coach has arrived, sir," the concierge assured us, as we stepped forward to meet the two men who turned out to be our Driver and Interpreter. As designated extrovert, I took over. Jabbering away at warp speed, I introduced us and showed the Driver and Interpreter my dog-eared map of Vietnam. Unlike Nick's Vietnam map, which even today, is still in mint condition, my map was already so beat up it was barely usable after only a week. I should point out that I am absolutely queer for maps, or any piece of paper that has any information on it whatsoever for that matter. And I am so detail-oriented that even my own kids won't ask me the simplest questions for fear of having to endure a two hour lecture.

I pointed out National Highway 14, which snaked up out of the lowlands to Dac Lac Province. Ultimately it led to the village Nick had operated out of during the war—Gia Nghia—which is now called Dak Nong. After I finished the introductions and my detailed list of instructions on the map, the Interpreter smiled, said "Yes," and motioned for us to get in the back seat of the Toyota, which was barely big enough for me, let alone the two of us. It was 6:15 a.m. and we were on our way. ～

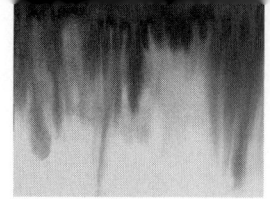

At This Rate, We'll Get There In Under Three Hours

As a well-traveled geography buff who has a world atlas next to each toilet in my house, I know that big maps of small countries can fool you into thinking that distances are further than they really are. I made a mental note, adjusting for that illusion which could easily fool a mere novice. The drive out of Saigon was swift and uneventful, save for the two hundred or so times we barely missed sideswiping a pedestrian, cyclist or motor scooter. And the motor scooters had two or three people riding on them. Often, a whole family rode on one. I don't know how the Vietnamese do it. Granted, they're generally small people—five foot two and a hundred and twenty pounds is a respectably fleshed-out adult. But I don't care how small you are. A family of four is not supposed to be able to ride on the same scooter. But they do. And they do it at relatively high speeds in dense, perplexing city traffic. We even saw a family of five riding on one scooter. Very impressive. Americans have created such a safety-crazed society, we must seem like complete wimps to the rest of the world when it comes to vehicular and urban safety. Fortunately, we offset this wimpish behavior by providing the excitement of random, sadistic violence on our city streets. Basically, I'd say it all comes out pretty even, but it's still unnerving when your driver brushes the skirt of a mother holding a baby on the back of a scooter in downtown Saigon. And in spite of their sometimes well-earned reputation for erratic driving in the U.S., the Vietnamese are gifted scooter drivers.

We accelerated smartly out of the city and crossed the span over the Saigon River. By the time we hit the first suburb, only thirty minutes had passed. We were really smoking now. And I do mean smoking. Unfortunately for Nick, both the Driver and the Interpreter chain-smoked. Among the three of us, Nick didn't stand a chance. All he could do was hang his head out the window, like the family dog. He waited for those precious moments when none of us were smoking, then he'd snap his head back into the car. He only played this game for about a half hour, when the bugs and the terrifying rush of oncoming traffic got the better of him. And, it seemed that the Driver came closer to hitting the oncoming traffic than he really had to.

It was difficult for us to predict how the Vietnamese would treat us. Our wives were particularly concerned for Nick, especially if the Vietnamese found out he had been a highly technically trained warrior in their country during the 60's. Usually they didn't know who Nick was or what he had been, but I suspected that both the Driver and Interpreter had been informed of these facts by my friend's brother, who knew the basic story. My friend had urged us, before we left, not to tell people that Nick had been a military advisor during the war, since government officials and village tyrants could make our trip inland unnecessarily difficult, if not downright dangerous. Our tour books also mentioned in passing that travel through Dac Lac Province, especially where we were headed, was still off limits, or at least discouraged, by the Vietnamese government.

The Rhade fought with the Americans against the Communists in the Vietnam War and especially in the "secret" CIA war in Laos during the same period. And after the war the Rhade continued to resist the Communist governments of Laos and Vietnam. There are only a few Rhade in Dac Lac, and the Vietnam government is a not overly concerned about them. But now, one of the guys who showed the Rhade how to use a bazooka was heading back up for an unannounced reunion thirty-five years later, and the government might get paranoid and overreact. More likely, some local cop or official would shake us down for a good cut of our cash.

Nick's natural introversion, and his seeming resolve to go to Dac Lac anyway, deepened his quiet reserve. I thought he wanted me to lay low and keep my big mouth under control for the day. More likely, he wanted me to shut my yap altogether. Of course, this is not easy for me to do. Regardless of Nick's wishes and our personal safety, I couldn't control myself. I *had* to talk. Besides, I almost felt like a real army guy as we started to ascend out of the coastal plain to the Highlands in the distance. The road was well-paved and it was clear sailing.

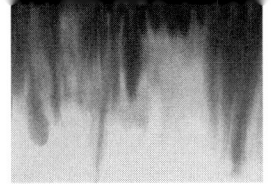

The Interpreter

An hour and a half had passed, and from the map I could tell we were half way to Gia Nghia. As we gained altitude, the temperature and humidity began to mercifully drop. The rice paddies gave way to a botanical no man's land of scrub brush and manioc. It was a very pleasant drive and I couldn't understand why, on this beautiful Saturday morning, there wasn't another car on the road. There was the inevitable procession of scooters and the occasional truck or bus, but no cars. Nick and I made some light, under-informed conversation on the geography and agriculture of the region while the Driver and the Interpreter chatted away in their native tongue. I thought it was time to find out who our escorts were and where they were from.

"Hey, where are you guys from?" I began. I waited for a response, but none came. I tried again. "Where are you from?"

The Interpreter clearly heard me this time. He turned to me, nodded, and then reached into his shirt pocket, pulled out his cigarettes and offered me one. Nick looked at me and offered a prophetic "Uh-oh," distinctly different from his usual HMM-HMM noises.

Well, it's not that the Interpreter knew no English. He just didn't know any English phrases or sentences. He did reassure us by showing us he had brought a Vietnamese-English reader along with him. The reader he had wasn't a translation dictionary, just a listing of life situations translated in English and Vietnamese. It was well-illustrated, but not indexed, so if you wanted to look up the Vietnamese word for "hotel," you couldn't find it unless you saw a drawing of it or got lucky after skimming through the pages for an hour. For the most part his reader was useful if you wanted to translate something like, "The French Exchequer is here to inspect your rice," but was completely useless if you wanted to say, "Stop the car, I'm going to puke." So that's the way it was going to be. The Interpreter couldn't speak English. This didn't seem to surprise or worry Nick at all. He just stared out the window, speaking less and less as we drove on. ~

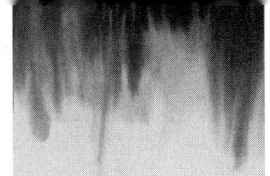

Something Really Stupid

THE NORTHERN AND SOUTHERN PARTS OF Vietnam are connected by two major arteries. The beautiful seaside highway follows the coast from Saigon to Hanoi. The train route parallels this highway. The other route is National Highway 14, which makes the north-south connection rather irregularly through the mountainous spine of the country, meandering inland near the borders of Cambodia and Laos. This route was parallel to, and at times during the "War against American imperialists and their puppet troops" part of, the Ho Chi Minh Trail. Throughout the war it was controlled by the Viet Cong. This explained why every time I asked Nick if he recognized "this hill" or "that river" along the road, he was clueless. Finally he told me he had never really driven on the roads and that all travel in the Central Highlands was by helicopter or fixed wing, single engine spotter planes. This statement, as simple and clinical as it seemed, floored me. It was the first time Nick had ever told me anything at all about his, or anyone else's experiences during the war. I seized the opportunity to extract some more information.

"Didn't you guys use the road to get around?," I carefully asked.

"Too dangerous and too stupid," he replied.

Too dangerous? He must be kidding! The whole damn war seemed to me to be a touch "dangerous" and a shitload of "stupid." I kept that thought to myself, not wanting to send him back into the "complete silence."

So I decided to lob a pebble across his bow instead. "What do you mean by 'stupid', Nick?"

"Well, Jim, we never put ourselves in any situation we couldn't control." Lesson One. As utterly violent and capriciously dangerous as it seemed, the American military intelligentsia, which certainly included Nick, never deliberately put themselves or their units in a "dangerous" or "stupid" situation. I never really knew that, or understood it in that way.

Nick interrupted my new, profound understanding of something in the war, with a provocative offering, "I've only done three stupid things in my life." Things began to spice up a bit for me now. "One time I had to get to a village very fast, and against my better judgment I drove a jeep, alone, for a mile on one of these roads."

I thought to myself—didn't that Korean War hero Hawkeye Pierce ride a jeep by himself all the time through enemy territory? Big deal.

"Okay, Nick, that was the stupidest thing you ever did, what was the second stupidest.?"

"No, Jim, that was the third most stupid. The second most stupid was flying as forward observer in a single engine plane two feet over the jungle canopy while I got peppered by the V.C. ground fire. The fuselage was full of holes but I saved my balls."

Now *that* did seem hairy. "How about the first?," I asked with great anticipation.

"Well, Jim, the number one stupidest goddamn thing I've ever done was to allow you to talk me into that motorcycle ride to Sa Pa."

Huh? He couldn't mean that sweet ride to the Tonkinese Alps. Apparently he did.

Four days earlier, Nick and I entered Vietnam through the northernmost part of the country, at the border with China. We had taken an overnight fourteen hour sleeper train from Kunming to the Chinese border town of Hekou. After being refused entrance to Vietnam the day of arrival, we finally got through the next morning. Once in Lao Cai, the Vietnamese border city, we hopped a ride to the train station to take the next train, which was the only practical way to get to Hanoi. In my Lonely Planet guidebook, there was an enticing entry about a small Montagnard village called Sa Pa, located high up in the nearby mountains. Nick's travel book, entitled "The Guide to the Most Expensive Hotels on the Planet," didn't mention Sa Pa, so my request came as a surprise to him.

"Let's try to get up to this little village in the Tonkinese Alps. My book says the road to it sucks but it sounds very remote and gorgeous."

I knew that the "very remote" comment would get Nick's testosterone pumping, because it meant some unique bragging rights for him when he related his travels to his more sedentary friends from Wall Street.

He nibbled on the bait. "Oh yeah? Let me take a look at that."

He read the entry on Sa Pa.

"This does sound interesting. But it says here that the road is so bad and the weather is usually so miserable that it might be faster to ride horses up the mountain. It also says you need at least three days to really see it and there's only one bus that goes up there each day."

Well, I knew damn well that travel guides always overdo it with their time requirements to properly see and appreciate an area or monument. "It is recommended that you allot three full days to explore the 'Temple of Tarry-Stool Bulimia' "the tour books would say. And guides like the Lonely Planet, whose regular readers have infinite time to spare, insist that you spend even more time to fully "experience" the temple.

"Bullshit," I told Nick. "If I could explore the entire Louvre *and* Eiffel Tower in one day, we sure as hell can get up to Sa Pa and back in one day."

The only problem was, the Vietnamese border officials held us up for three hours and by the time we got to the train/bus station, the one bus to Sa Pa had already left. I was down, but not out.

Out in the dusty street, I looked for someone who spoke English. I found a German student, the only other white person I could find. He said he had just spent a week in Sa Pa and yes, when the weather breaks, the scenery is spectacular, but the road up the mountain was horrific and there were even some bandits. I asked him if he would recommend riding on the back of a hired motorcycle. He said those guys *were* the bandits. Besides, the road had sheer drop-offs, no shoulders, water buffalo and snakes everywhere, and the bridges were not exactly what you find in Madison County. This conversation was just too much for me to bear. I called to Nick, who was crouching down and saying something to a small child.

"Nick, the weather is clearing and I've just found out the road to Sa Pa is quite good, recently repaved, I understand. Let's go, we'll get the night train to Hanoi."

Nick balked. "How? The bus has gone already."

"Wait here a second," I said confidently.

Two minutes later I had commandeered Russian-made motorcycles from two guys on the street. I asked one of them if he would drive me up to Sa Pa on the back of the motorcycle. As I hand-gestured my request to him, his eyes widened, then he dropped, like an animal taking a bullet. On the ground, he started to belly laugh uncontrollably. We were quickly surrounded by a crowd of villagers. I knew what would come next.

First I got patted on the gut. Then my ass. Then the group grope commenced, like the one Richard Dreyfus experienced in "Close Encounters of the Third Kind". My size was so alien to the Vietnamese that they had to touch me to confirm that their sense of sight was not playing tricks.

The Vietnamese, like other Asians I had come in contact with over the years, seem mesmerized by big people. And I was as big as some entire families put together. They were particularly interested in my weight in kilograms. As I counted off 130 kg on my fingers, 5 kg at a time, they would gasp and give me a rousing applause. At times, I would catch a glimpse of Nick, always standing well off to the side, alone. This time, he was clapping along with the crowd. After taking a bow for achieving such an admirable size, I turned back to the motorcyclist and the business at hand. No, his motorcycle couldn't get us both up the mountain. But yes, for five bucks a day, Nick and I could lease his and his friend's motorcycles.

With everyone in town watching and with no time to think, Nick had no choice but to hop on his motorcycle. I hopped on mine, kicked the starter, and fired down the dirt road. The crowd loved watching my two ax handle ass disappear in a cloud of smoke and dust. Several miles later I checked the rear view mirror. No Nick. I turned around and sped back to the parking lot at the train station. The crowd had not dispersed and actually seemed to be bigger. Still no Nick. Then, exploding through the scattering crowd, Nick came flying. He swerved, dropped into a rut, hit the brakes, then the accelerator, which made him pop a wheelie. Wow! He was good and the crowd loved it. He then roared by me and screamed "Where are the FUCK-ING brakes?" I caught up to him and motioned to him to hit the right front pedal and left hand brake. In the confusion of the moment he did exactly the opposite, jamming the motorcycle into first gear while gunning the engine. While the justifiably concerned owner of the motorcycle chased after us, I urged Nick to keep going until we crossed the bridge over the Red River.

When we outran the owner and the exuberant crowd, I motioned to Nick to stop. He turned off the ignition key, the engine died, and he coasted to a stop.

"Goddamn it, Jim. If I die today, your sister-in-law will strangle you herself," he said with no humor in his voice whatsoever.

It seemed odd to me that through all the battle training with planes and tanks and true grit that Nick had missed training on one particularly useful vehicle.

"Jeezus, Nick, when's the last time you were on a motorcycle?" I asked with true, but incredulous concern.

"This *is* my first time you son of a bitch! Let's call a cab."

I threatened to tell his sons, my son, and the other important guys that he, the toughest bastard any of us knew, was a fraidy cat. Well, at that moment, Nick made the Number One stupidest decision of his life. He listened to me.

It took us a while to negotiate our motorcycles up that mountain road. Yes, we had no helmets. Yes, the bridges were either out, or made of pick-up sticks, and we had to ford the streams through the water. Yes, we ran over poisonous snakes and nearly had head-on collisions with water buffalo that made us look like ants. But on that day, when every curve was steep, I saw a guy transfixed in competition with himself, revealing a truly steep learning curve on a motorcycle. On the way up the mountain, he was an accident waiting to happen. By the time we headed down the mountain later that incredible afternoon, he was Evel Knievel, roaring past me, turning his inside knee and shoulder into the pavement as he negotiated high speed turns. What a stud.

Five minutes later I caught up with him. He was stopped in the middle of the road. I pulled up. We then witnessed something unusual. An enormous water buffalo was inching across the road. Amazingly, he was being coaxed along by a microscopic toddler, no more than two years old. The naked child led the buffalo, holding onto a nose ring. When they got to the other side of the road and stepped into the ditch next to a terrained rice paddy, the kid held on to the ring as the buffalo's stride raised to step over the ditch. This tiny kid just held on as he was jerked off his feet into the air. He hung on for dear life until the bull finally lowered him down into the mud. The child just whispered something to the beast, who lumbered on, obediently following the child. I was certain that if the bull had even sneezed, the kid would have been launched across the rice paddy. But the little child, who could barely walk, was in complete control. The scene was bewildering and I was dumbfounded. Nick, on the other hand, just stood there watching with a kindly, knowing look. To this day, I suspect he knew or felt something I hadn't quite grasped yet.

The decision to ride the motorcycles up to Sa Pa that day may have been something really stupid that he agreed to do, but I swear Nick had a different kind of smile on his face the rest of the drive down that mountain.

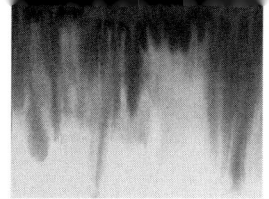

The Road to Gia Nghia

THE BITTERSWEET REMEMBRANCES OF STUPID, irresponsible acts were interrupted by a noticeable change in the quality of the road. What started out as the highway of dreams rudely degenerated into Dante's hell hole. Sometimes one is so shocked not by how absolutely bad something is, but rather by how short it comes up relative to something else that seems a bit better. Not in this case. This segment of National Highway 14 was not relatively bad. It was absolutely bad. And after a mile it was starting to become pretty unbearable.

"I'll be damn glad when we get through this piece of road", I yelled to the Interpreter.

Between the frightening noises that were being generated by the interactions of car and "road," and the complete inability of the Interpreter to understand anything I said, conversation was futile. The violent up and down and side to side gyrations were reminiscent of another road I'd experienced—the dreaded B3 in Kenya.

The B3, which connects the central highlands of Kenya down the steep escarpment to the Rift Valley below, was built by the Italians after World War II. As that once sound track began to crumble in the 1970's it was repaved with a substance the consistency of ear wax. I swear you can actually *see* the surface of the B3 flowing down hill before your eyes. I thought I'd seen the worst. And semi-yearly repaving didn't help. Ultimately, the roadbed of the B3 gave way, creating potholes that gobbled up unwary vehicles, like a Venus Fly Trap closing in over a bug. I thought of my wife who'd spent a year in physical therapy for her back after only two rides on the B3. Kenya was her last trip to the Third World. No more Third World trips for her until they fixed their roads.

National Highway 14 in Vietnam seemed hell-bent on vying with the B3 for the "Worst Road in All Four Hemispheres" award. And like the B3, the road to Gia Nghia was widened by vehicles that kept creeping further and further into the brush on the side of the road. The only sane way to drive was to ride with one wheel in the bush and one wheel on a ridge of stones. In this way, one could also slalom around and avoid large rocks which, depending on the clearance of your vehicle, would otherwise destroy the undercarriage of your car.

The only problem was that on this road a Toyota offered virtually zero clearance. We were constantly clunking over rocks that, in spite of being benign to trucks, were creating a frightening racket in a car that had no business being on this road. Why did my friend's brother send us off on a trek in a car he must have known was no match for this road? I could only guess that since the road ate Toyotas for lunch, we were to be part of some higher mission of which we were totally unaware. Perhaps, once a month, a 1987 Toyota was offered up as a sacrifice to appease the Highland gods.

On another trip we might have called it quits at this point. I was sure that the intensity of the body slams we were taking could detach some of our major organ systems. Re-attaching floating kidneys is not a pretty surgical procedure. A much worse possibility would be developing the dreaded "old man's dangling nuts" syndrome. Our whirligigs were taking quite a beating on this road and since I had been vasectomized, those charming little adhesions you develop on the sweet spot of your family jewels were really singing with each jolt on this road. I glanced over at Nick for some empathy but, as usual, he was poker-faced. But I could tell he was also feeling some pangs, since he was allowing something to happen that, unless it was in a combat situation, two guys would never allow to happen—our knees were actually touching. When this went on for more than five seconds, I knew we were on a really serious mission and there was no turning back. But there seemed to be something happening with the car and the road that was utterly unnecessary.

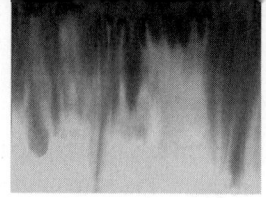

The Driver

"THERE'S SOMETHING UTTERLY UNNECESSARY goin' on here" I thought to myself as I shared my suspicions with Nick.

"Yeah, I started noticing it about an hour ago," Nick said in a tone that reflected that he, too, had a stranglehold on the obvious.

"What the hell's wrong with this guy?" I asked with genuine curiosity.

"Maybe he's pissed because he's missing the Knick's game," Nick offered, referring to one of the zillions of meaningless playoff games we were all missing today.

"He's mad about something. I'd be pissed too if I was forced into driving on this piece of shit road," I added, trying to give him some benefit of the doubt.

It's not as if the road wasn't bad enough. It seemed as if the Driver was going out of his way to run the tires over the largest rocks in the road. He would swerve off course and—slam!—the car would be lifted off its moorings as we ran right over the points of the rocks. At other times, he would take dead aim and run the center of the drive train directly over rocks that we obviously couldn't clear. The racket was unbelievable. To top it off, he violated the first rule for driving on thoroughfares like the Kenyan B3 or Vietnamese Highway 14. You *never, ever* drive in the middle of the road.

Sure, in morning traffic in Saigon, he did seem to lack a certain finesse at the wheel. But this present behavior was suicidal and we were certain to end up doing eggbeaters, end over end, at some point in the journey. At best we'd end up stranded in the Highlands for a few days. There were a lot of things wrong with that option. What the hell was wrong with this guy?

I studied his moves very carefully for about thirty minutes. During this time even the Interpreter was berating him for his seeming recklessness. It was obvious that the Driver wasn't really reckless at all. Whatever he was doing, he really meant it. Then, through the rear view mirror, I noticed that he was concentrating intensely just before he hit each rock on the road. Nick saw it too.

At once we both realized the bizarre truth. We had been sent off to a remote village in Dac Lac Province in the Central Highlands with an Interpreter who couldn't speak English or Rhade, in a car that was no match for even the best part of the road, with a Driver who was virtually blind. The world he saw through his eyes was shifted ten degrees off of where the world really was. He lived in a visual world where parallax ruled the day. And now we were part of that off-center world.

And the Toyota was not enjoying the ride at all.

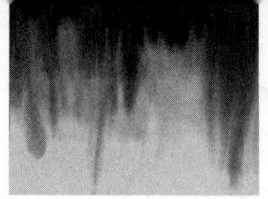

Name That Tune

Two hours passed since we got off the paved part of the road and we were finally rattled into a state of full-body anesthesia. Then, just when we had become habituated to the mind-numbing jolts, we turned a corner and—thank you, sweet Jesus—we were back on a hard road. This new, beautifully engineered, paved road was actually the main street leading into a small town. The buildings were surprisingly well-built. On each building proudly hung a red Communist Party national flag out a second story window. Apparently, this had originally been a loyalist Viet Cong village in the decidedly anti-Communist province of Dac Lac. And the rewards the townspeople enjoyed lasted exactly one kilometer through the center of town. At the edge of town, we were back on the Path of Pain. We needed something to desensitize our completely bruised corpses again.

"Okay Nick, how 'bout this one?" I began, "Ram-doo-da-ooh da dit dah-wa, wa."

Nick struggled. "The Beatles?"

I had him for the tenth straight time. "Wrong again, Nick—that was by Willie Dixon."

It was Nick's turn. "Don-don-don-ta-don. Don, don, don, dona-don."

Now it was my turn to struggle. "Beethoven?"

He chuckled smugly at me. "Not even close, Jim. That's by Rubenstein. You're zero for ten."

As usual, our game of "Name that Musician" continued on, with neither of us ever getting close to guessing the other's tune. Nick only knows classical music. I know absolutely no classical music. He knew that as long as he never used a Beethoven riff, I'd never score a point. In stark contrast, Nick knows no modern music whatsoever, unless it's a show tune from a Barbara Streisand or Julie Andrews musical. So I just kept to blues, rock, and fusion tunes, to which he'd inevitably answer, "The Beatles," which of course, was never the right answer. In the end, we tied at zero-zero, except for one asterisk win by Nick in a bar in Bali that is still under protest from me.

The flat tire arrived unceremoniously, with the quiet hiss of a cleric passing gas. The Driver pulled to the side of the road, sideswiping a log in front of a grass hut just for good measure. We were at a sharp turn in the road, but there was such little traffic at this point, I decided not to protest the Driver's poor choice of location for his pit stop.

While the Driver and Interpreter attended to the infirm tire, Nick walked with slow, measured steps toward the hut. Peering outside the hut was a topless woman, with nipples as black and shiny as obsidian. The scene had a decidedly preliterate air about it. I then caught a glimpse inside the dark interior of the one-roomed stilt house, where a family sat on the floor eating lunch. As Nick slowly approached, two toddlers came out of the hut and waved at him, grinning from ear to ear. Nick beckoned to them, but they abruptly turned and went back into the hut, as if being called inside. At that moment I became aware of a group of distant voices, chanting in an oddly recognizable language. Around the corner came a procession of forty or fifty people. The first person was carrying a large wooden cross, and in the middle of the funeral march, men were pulling a two-wheeled cart. On the cart was a casket with a swastika painted on it. They continued to chant the funeral dirge as they passed by us.

"What's that language?" I whispered to Nick, hoping his classical training would pay off.

"It's Latin, with a touch of Rhade woven in." When they passed out of earshot Nick continued, explaining that the Rhade were schooled in Latin and Catholicism by French missionaries in the middle of this century. And by the end of the mid 1950's the Rhade began their emergence from the Iron Age with the creation of their first written language. Although useful, this began a long and bittersweet exposure of the Rhade to the West and the rest of the world. And I suspect the devastation of Rhade culture has been a much more bitter, than sweet, experience to them.

The Driver and Interpreter had finished changing the tire and we got back into the Toyota. The Interpreter said something very serious to the Driver. I'm sure he said something close to, "Okay eagle eye—we're out of spares—try harder." As we pulled off, I looked over at Nick who was waving to the two kids. He turned back to me and asked, "I couldn't make out what was written on the cross. Did you catch it?"

"Yeah, Nick, it had an inscription on it, probably a name. And the dates 1984-1996 were carved into it."

Nick looked out the window.

"Christ, that was a 12 year old in that casket. I wonder what happened," I asked.

Nick did not utter a word for another hour of the drive to Gia Nghia. ~

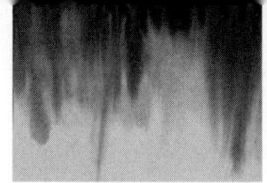

Elephant Crossing

We were five and a half hours into the ride and the Toyota was beginning to display some disquieting symptoms. The drive train started to make a few randomly timed clicking noises. The exhaust system was showing signs of coming loose at the seams. And, not that it mattered much to the Driver, but the response of the steering wheel was losing a certain crispness.

We were all at that point in any trip when everyone falls into a trance. Not a defocused profound Zen state, mind you, but a type of 30 IQ dullness that salmon must experience when they're nearing their destiny, exhausted in the shallow headwater of their demise. This knuckle-headed dullness was broken as we rounded a turn and the Interpreter screamed something at the Driver. The Driver correctly decoded the scream and slammed on the brakes.

We spun to a stop in a cloud of red dust. As the air cleared we saw, up close and personal, what had so motivated the Interpreter to yell. We were knee high to the pointy end of a bull elephant ambling up the road.

This actually brought Nick out of his own trance. "Now *there's* a vehicle with proper clearance for this road."

"Yeah, unless he's draggin' some morning wood," was my own wise-ass retort.

The Interpreter pointed to the opposite side of the road to the Driver, who carefully followed the Interpreter's instructions to negotiate the Toyota around the beast. As we prayed for the only four tires we had to remain pressurized, the Driver accelerated and we were off again.

I took the opportunity in this break in the non-action to engage Nick.

"Did you run into any elephants or tigers when you were here in '67?" I asked Nick as if he had been here on a photo safari.

Nick paused. "Only from the air. The animals generally sat out the war."

I liked his answer and pressed on. As we drove further into the Highlands, the jungle became much denser, although in recent years much of it adjacent to the road had been cleared for rubber trees and coffee bushes. Still, one could appreciate how thick the vegetation was and how completely impossible it would have been to see any animals or troop movements. I then realized that pictures and movies really didn't do it any justice at all.

I approached the issue gingerly. "How the hell did you guys see the enemy in this bullshit?"

Nick looked out the car window and didn't say a word. I was pushing him and he didn't seem pleased. We drove on.

Ten minutes, which seemed like two hours, went by. Still looking out the window, Nick said, "Okay."

"What's that Nick?" I didn't know what he would say next, but I wasn't hopeful. Then he broke his silence.

"My orders were to intercept and destroy supply lines coming down the trail from the North," he began.

"By yourself?" I responded with expert military savvy.

He was patient with me.

"Units of six to fifteen." He continued his descriptions.

As an advisor on infantry tactics, Nick had to train the Rhade in modern guerrilla warfare and lead them through this opaque foliage to seek out and destroy units of Viet Cong supply lines. This could not have been a picnic, especially since the Rhade, who were otherwise wonderful, warm people, never proved to take well to guns, bazookas, grenades or mortar shells. Apparently, they aimed these weapons about as well as the Driver aimed our Toyota.

Nick continued his account of the hardware and strategies they used to pick apart the Ho Chi Minh Trail. His explanation was technically detailed and I was, of course, fascinated. Like other anti-war guys, I am completely enthralled and mesmerized by things that go boom. And his experiences at ground level were enhanced by the unimaginable bomb barrage the trail took from 40,000 feet above. But most of all, hearing his descriptions and seeing that jungle up close, in 3D, finally put to rest any residual boyhood daydreams I had that any of it was fun. And Nick hadn't talked about any of the real thing. Yet.

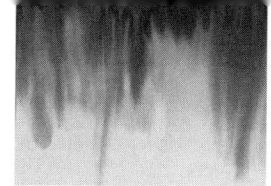

What's Worse Than War?

NICK'S "WEAPONS AND TECHNOLOGIES OF WAR" seminar made the next hour of our rock and roll mogul ride to Gia Nghia pass very quickly, indeed. Even the Driver and the Interpreter, who didn't understand one iota of what Nick was saying, seemed to hang on to his every word. The Driver stared intently at Nick's reflection in the rear view mirror, completely ignoring the road. This actually improved the ride, until we clipped the ass of a dog who was napping on the road. The dog did a half spin and limped off into the brush. Nick became very upset at the dog's race career-ending, but non-fatal, collision. He went silent again.

I tried the one sure tactic I thought might induce him into more storytelling. I started a political argument with him. This was a bit risky, seeing as we didn't have any booze, which we normally used to act as the ultimate arbiter and mediator of truth in our political arguments, which always ended in a drunken stalemate. Bravely, I pushed on without the benefit of the safety net.

"Did you believe in the war the whole time you were here?" I began.

"Yes and I still do."

"We lost, Nick," I said recklessly. "And haven't we all decided it was a bad idea anyway? "

Nick paused and then explained his position.

"When I entered Vietnam in January 1967, an infantry colonel who had fought in Korea conducted the first in-country briefing for the group of U.S. soldiers that had arrived with me. He told us he knew we had heard from many in the United States that Vietnam was the wrong war, in the wrong place, at the wrong time; that America had no business butting in to defend a reluctant country against communism; that the Vietnamese people were corrupt, poorly motivated, and not capable of being trained to defend themselves. He went on to say that many people in America had felt the same about the Korean War and the Korean people in 1950 when he was leaving the U.S. to fight there. He could tell us from his own personal experience that the South Vietnamese were less corrupt, more freedom loving and democratic, more motivated, better led, and more trainable than the South Koreans had been in 1950. He concluded that if Americans had the will to win, and if we did our jobs as well as American soldiers had during the Korean War, then we would prevail—the South Vietnamese people would be saved from the horrible fate that had fallen upon the North Vietnamese people after the French left; they would remain free, strengthen their democracy, and flourish as the South Koreans had since the end of their war. And what's more, if we prevailed, we would save millions in Laos, Cambodia, and, perhaps, the rest of Southeast Asia, from the ravages of what communist aggression would surely inflict on them if we did not. I thought that was a compelling argument in '67, Jim, and do you know what—even jaded by the fact that we did not prevail, that we lost the war, I don't find fault with that colonel's argument today. Every time I play it back in my mind, and I still do that a lot, I find it persuasive. I'll bet that just blows your mind, doesn't it, Jim? And here's what blows mine. Sometimes it seems to me that the only reason that this nation feels good about its role in the Korean War, and regrets its role in the Vietnam War, is because we won in Korea and lost in Vietnam."

Nick paused. I was amazed that he was able to put together such a succinct monologue on cue. Perhaps he had run it through his psyche many times over the years. He continued.

"In spite of all that, Jim, I'm not convinced that the U.S. involvement in Vietnam was a total failure. Maybe it's just rationalization, maybe I just can't admit that 50,000 American lives, some of them my friends and classmates, were lost in vain. If you look at Vietnam as just one part of a much larger process, you can conclude that the cumulative weight of all the separate parts did, in the end, prevail. The individual battles of Korea in the 1950's, the British success in Malaysia, the indigenous resistance to communist takeovers in Indonesia, and in the Philippines, our struggle in Vietnam, and all the singular struggles against the communists in Southeast Asia in the 20th century, whether victorious at the time, made a contribution in the end."

He did have a point there, but his argument still had an air of hand waving to it. To me, Nick has a purely practical approach to politics. You know, if a policy or law or principle doesn't work at first, get rid of it. And I told him so, in spite of the fact that his reading material for the trip was not Jack Kerouac, but rather DeToqueville's "Democracy in America." Nevertheless I told Nick that he was not driven by central principles of political thought, only their practical outcomes. But God bless them, while some of us are burning daylight deep in principled thought, the Nicks are out there really changing the world. I refused to pay him the compliment, probably because my balls were aching so from the jarring we were taking. I decided to end-run him by groveling for some sympathy.

"I also felt isolated during the war, you know." It was a weak attempt but it did continue the conversation.

"What the hell are you talking about? You protesters had 20 percent of the country with you. That wasn't exactly loneliness, especially on the goddamn campuses." Nick was obviously not impressed by this approach.

The truth was I really didn't know anyone then who actually shared my attitude. Most of the students I knew were either right wing, knee-jerk hawks, or left wing dreamers who were into socialism. I was against the war, but I really despised collectivism in all forms. But anyway, my libertarian bullets completely failed to penetrate Nick's armor.

Then it hit me, right through my frontal lobes. I was now ready for my knockout punch on Nick's continued support of America's intervention in Vietnam's ageless civil war.

"Nick, don't get me wrong. War is not the worst thing that can happen."

"Oh *really*, Jim?" He thought I had surrendered.

"I always believed in Gandhi's angle on war." I was being honest here. "You know, the highest level is passive resistance. War is regrettable, but not the worst alternative to passive resistance."

"Okay, Jim. I give up. What's the alternative worse than war? "

I think Nick knew the answer, but didn't want to spoil my fun.

"Doing nothing at all. Just pure, ass-kissing pacifism." And this is what really frosted me about my pacifist comrades throughout the war and for many years afterward. I thought they refused to stand up to anyone for any real principles they understood and believed in. What's worse, they were willing to hand it all over to the biggest losers of all time, the Marxists.

Nick nodded.

That was it. After thirty years of total disagreement on everything, we finally stood on a tiny speck of common ground. ⌇

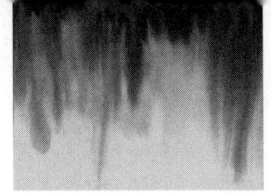

Gettin' Laid In That Pond At Woodstock

From what I could tell, we were getting pretty close to Gia Nghia. The ride that should have taken two and one-half hours had now passed the seven hour mark. Finally we turned off the Road of a Thousand Tortures and continued on a "secondary" road that was actually an improvement. We only had $1/32$ of an inch of map left to drive, and we'd be in Gia Nghia.

I tried to enjoy the compelling scenery, but my mind wandered. I had a hunch that neither Nick's nor my precis of the World of War really hit the mark, other than to elevate our personal opinions to sound bite status. The raw fact remained that he was here, and I wasn't. And my convictions as a kid in the 60's and 70's, as sincere as they were, were tucked into bed safe and sound each night. Nick's moral convictions may have experienced a bit more insomnia than mine. But I couldn't worry about that. My mind cleared and I began to concentrate on more important issues, like where and when we could score some beer. I had the hardest time communicating this to the Interpreter. From the back seat I acted out the concept "I want a cold beer" to him. I did five minutes of charades, holding my arms wrapped around my body, shivering, and chugging down an imaginary can and rubbing my belly in satisfaction. I was convinced I was acting out the accepted International Symbol for ordering a cold beer. Instead, he offered me a malaria pill and a cigarette. I declined the pill, took the cigarette, and forgot about getting a beer of any temperature, until we got to Gia Nghia.

Nick interrupted my important twenty-fifth cigarette of the day with a comment that came from out of the blue.

"Did you ever do anything in your life that you regret you did?"

In spite of the fact that the trauma of the morning's ride had permanently detached all but the most important synapses in my brain, I realized the seriousness of the question. I gave it some careful thought. After several minutes of earnest deliberation, I answered him with a most thoroughly unsatisfactory answer.

"No."

My answer was, of course, a conversation ender. I should have given Nick something much better to work with. He wanted to tell me something but I completely stuffed him under the basket with my answer. So I just started to ramble on about how I grew up as a scrupulously pure Catholic boy and that, as a pubescent soldier of Christ, I had even been chosen "Catholic Boy of the Year," and that had somehow earned me the honor of meeting Nelson Rockefeller. To this day I still don't get the linkage of those events, but I rambled on to Nick about how I bought *The Baltimore Catechism* lock, stock and barrel, and how the only sins I ever told in Confession were "sins against the symmetry of the universe," which few priests were able to cope with, especially coming from an eight year old. I pulled it all together by telling him, quite honestly, and not proud to admit, that I never lied, cheated or stole. I tried to relate to Nick that no, I never did anything that I regretted or was ashamed of. I think he really believed me because he gave me that same look of sympathetic surprise that Andy Griffith saved on special occasions for Barney Fife when he said something particularly naive and pitiful. And this was coming from another goody-two shoes, Italian-American Catholic boy, who I considered the second most genuinely moral, ethical person I ever knew. And he kept those ethics while simultaneously making a ton of money as an investment banker. So considering the Nick I know, I couldn't imagine what he was getting at with his question.

Nick looked straight ahead for a moment, then he turned to me.

As he opened his mouth to speak, the Interpreter opened up a hot can of Coke that he had been saving and that had been getting agitating in the floor well of his shotgun seat. The can opened with a hearty "pop!" and Nick jolted up out of his seat and, in a blur, he ducked into the small well in front of his own seat. Reacting to Nick, I straightened up, hitting my head on the ceiling. The Driver and the Interpreter began to guffaw. At that moment, the Toyota navigated a turn, and spread out before us was one of the most serene looking towns I'd ever seen. It was Gia Nghia.

Nick motioned to the Driver to stop the car. Nick and I got out and took in, in our own different ways, the beautiful setting. Nick took a deep breath, sighed, and got back into the Toyota. I followed. But I had developed a strong need for closure to our conversation. I spilled my guts out to him.

"Nick, there is one thing in my life I regret. Remember that scene at Woodstock where there was a group of naked kids in the pond, hugging and smokin' dope and gettin' laid."

"Oh, yeah." Even Nick appreciated that scene.

"Well, I was working at a Summer Stock Theater near Woodstock that weekend. And when it came time to blow off work and sneak off to the concert, I decided, instead, to stay at work. I do dearly regret not gettin' laid at that pond in Woodstock?" ∼

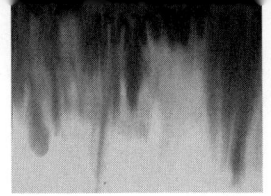

So Close, Yet So Far

GIA NGHIA IS SET ON, AND BETWEEN, A CLUSTER of hills and valleys that rises from the plateau that defines the Central Highlands. Looking at the distant town from the road, I could swear we were in the Berkshire Mountains of western Massachusetts, or perhaps the Green Mountains of Vermont. As we drove closer to the edge of town, we reached the final hurdle of the ride. By this time the Toyota's steering mechanism was so loose that the Driver had to rotate the steering wheel at least a half turn before the wheels began to turn at all. The exhaust system had broken loose in several places, creating a guttural muffler noise that suggested that the engine possessed some actual horsepower, which it didn't have anymore. The drive train clunks were actually the scariest noises, but these were partially drowned out by new rattles, which reflected the fact that every rivet, bolt, and screw in the Toyota was loosening. Now, in the last stretch into Gia Nghia, a brand new layer of sharp stones, the size of papayas, covered the road. There was no way around this stretch of road, which was sure to put the fatal holes in our only tires. Undeterred, the Driver inched through the last minefield until we successfully reached the town.

"Well, Nick, has the place changed at all?"

"I have no idea," he said. "I've never been in this place before."

This admission did not sit well with me. I quickly got the map out and assured Nick that this must be the place. He then rolled down his window and held his head outside as we headed for downtown. Finally it hit him.

"Wait . . . This is the place."

Nick insisted that although visually he couldn't recognize a damn thing, the sounds of the town, and especially the smells, were unmistakable. These memories were welling up from deep in his belly, and I didn't question his observations.

As we drove into town, the heads of the locals were really snapping. Most of the populace had not seen a white person since 1973. There were no TV antennas to be seen, even after the Montagnard stilt houses gave way to the sturdier structures of the town itself.

We tried to direct the Interpreter to different parts of town, but he had the Driver follow a predetermined route, with the surprisingly confident assurance of a local. He sure seemed to know where he was going, but it would have been nice if he let us in on where he was taking us. At this point I asked Nick an important question.

"Nick, do we have a—a—destination?"

His answer was less than gratifying. "No, I just came up for a look. We can go back to Saigon now."

"WHAT?" I said in a tone louder than the exploding Coke can. "We've got to do *something,* see *something,* see *someone* up here," I pleaded. "There must be someone you knew who might still be here."

"I doubt it, Jim."

He was starting to really frustrate me now. He had jerked my chain at other times on this trip. At least it seemed that way. Maybe he was being straight with me the whole time, but if he was, then I really don't understand him at all.

Two months earlier, when we had to decide what kind of videos and cameras to bring on the trip, he said, "None. It's the actual experience that's important—pictures just don't cut it." I love to take videos on my trips but he nixed that idea, claiming people posed and spoke artificially for video. He wanted no photographic record whatsoever. I politicked him heavily, just to bring a couple of disposable cameras with us. And other than taking pictures of him in front of Asian banks, municipal building projects, and the like, I was always talked out of bringing a camera on our best side trips. So other than a few dozen shots of Nick standing at attention in front of a building I cared nothing about, and in which he always looked like a military advisor, we have no pictorial record of our trip.

His reluctant and critical opinion of photographs, which didn't reflect the "actions of the experience," was rendered totally incomprehensible to me by his actual behavior during the "actions of the experience." You could bring this horse to water, but no, he wouldn't drink. When we visited China Beach, I frolicked on the beach while he stood on the grass, well away from the beach. When we hiked to an impressive waterfall that exploded into a beautiful pool in the jungle, I ran into the waterfall while he watched. And later, in Bali, when I went body surfing in the waves, Nick viewed the surf from poolside while keeping one eye on his money. (Later, I read his notes on this experience, which read "Jim goes swimming while I watch *our* money.") And now that we had finally reached Gia Nghia, ground zero itself, he walked to the brink, saw enough, and was ready to go home. It was as if whatever "experience" he was having privately, in his mind, from memory triggered by the sights and smells and sounds was enough for him. And he didn't mind leaving me out of it. No way, Nick. Not this time. We're going on, buddy.

"There must be someone you'd like to say 'hi' to. C'mon, Nick, try to remember," I begged, but he remained still.

After a few minutes of driving, we neared the market, which defined the center of town. As we pulled up, Nick quietly said, "There is one person I wouldn't mind seeing again." Finally we had something to work with.

"Who is he Nick?" I asked.

"Actually, he's a she. Her name is Heman or H'Moun, or something like that."

"What's her first name?"

"That is her first name," Nick said. "I don't remember her last name."

Oh, great. This was going to be real easy. Just like walking into Ames, Iowa, and asking if George, who lived there thirty years ago, was still hanging around town.

"C'mon Nick, you must remember something that can help us locate her."

"Actually, I don't want to go around looking for her anyway. We screwed up her life pretty good last time the Americans came to town. If it's all the same to you, I'm not up for doing it to her again."

"That was thirty years ago, Nick. What's the problem?"

"When the Viet Cong took over they didn't treat her very kindly for that. Let's not remind everyone about that now—if she's still alive."

Before I could extract another factoid from Nick, the Driver pulled up next to the market area and the Interpreter urged us to get out of the car. He motioned for us to follow him into the market.

Why not? Maybe we'd find a cold beer somewhere. But we were already running out of time, and the probability of finding this woman, or a cold beer, in this town, was rapidly approaching zero.

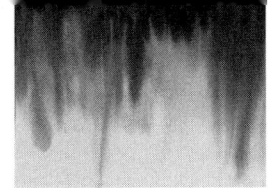

*Toi Muon Lam Tinh Voi
Tat Ca Dan Ba Trong Lang*

THE MARKETPLACE IN GIA NGHIA WAS QUITE large, especially when compared to the size of the town itself. It was also more laid back than those found on the coast or in the more touristy cities of Vietnam, which is to say, *any* other city in Vietnam. The vendors in the outdoor market were snoozing in hammocks over their wares. Being a regional capital, the Gia Nghia market attracted farmers, vendors, and customers from a healthy-sized swath of the provinces. But this was siesta time. That is, until Nick and I walked through the place. The whole market came alive immediately. Nick and I knew what would happen next. First, came the "look at the white guys!" jaw drops, then the giggles, then the laying on of hands and the inevitable belly rubs. Nick was always left out of these crowd scenes around me, but he seemed to enjoy the show thoroughly anyway.

This time, however, when we followed the Interpreter into the inner sanctum of the market, I was pleasantly overrun by a veritable swarm of 18-25 year old women, who couldn't keep their hands off of me. Nick, who is very fond of the Vietnamese and Montagnard people, finds the women absolutely irresistible. Now he was jealous.

"Nick, quick, where's that piece of paper I gave you yesterday?"

He fumbled in his pockets for a second. "Why do you want it—are you sick?" He handed it to me.

Days before, I had a concierge translate something for me and write it out in Vietnamese. It went "Toi muon lam tinh voi tat ca dan ba trong lang." Although Nick learned some Vietnamese back in 1966 at the Army Language School, he didn't even know how to say "hi" in Vietnamese now, let alone understand this phrase. I told him it meant, "Take me to the hospital. I feel very ill," and that it would come in very handy in a bad situation.

In this situation, I didn't appear very ill to him, and quite the contrary, Nick definitely wished he was in my shoes at the moment. I asked him to hand the paper to some important looking older males in the market. The Interpreter wedged his way through the women, who were all over me by now. He pointed to the young ladies' ring fingers and whispered to me "Married—no,no." He was right. Most of the women were married and the interested men in the background were probably their husbands. In a moment of clarity I yelled to Nick.

"Forget it Nick, I need the piece of paper back." Nick just shook his head and handed it back to me. I then excused myself politely, but firmly, from the group-grope and followed the Interpreter to a stall further down the aisle. He introduced us to a young woman he knew very well. After some animated gestures, the Interpreter told us he had been stationed here, in Gia Nghia, for three years as either a land surveyor or a peeping Tom, but I couldn't quite decipher which one. This was good news to us. Now it made at least some sense as to why he was sent along as our Interpreter.

After meeting his friends, the Interpreter led us out of the indoor market and pointed across the street to a cafe. We followed.

As we walked to the cafe, Nick asked me "What was that all about back there—you didn't look to sick to me."

I figured I better let him know what I was up to, so we wouldn't make a dangerous mistake the next time I had an urge to bust his balls just for fun.

"That note isn't really related to going to the hospital at all. But I guess that's where it could have sent us," I told him.

"What do you mean?"

"Well, Nick, it seemed like a good idea at the time—but my good sense prevailed."

"What did the note say, for Christ's sake?"

"I want to have sex with all the women in your village," I confessed.

"Hey, that reminds me...." he started.

Without missing a beat I finished his sentence. "I know. I wonder if your friend Heman is somewhere around here?"

"No, that's not what I meant," he said.

Sure, Nick, I thought. You can't bullshit a bullshitter.

We had reached the cafe. ∼

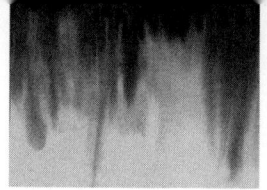

Cold Beer

THE CAFE WAS A ONE ROOM, CONCRETE floored box that would make a minimalist's mouth water. There were several sets of tables and stools that were exactly half as high and half as wide as they needed to be for me to sit down. I was able to support myself by putting three stools together—one on each cheek and one for spillage. Being the naturally well-bred, decorum-loving, goodwill ambassador that I am, I sat down and immediately screamed for a cold beer. This got no response from the owner/waiter, so I motioned to the Interpreter to go to the car and get his Vietnamese-English "translator". I was desperately thirsty and couldn't wait for the Interpreter to get back with his book, let alone spend the time leafing through the pages for French Exchequer rice inspection dialogue. So I immediately went in to my pantomime routine, acting out the International Cold Beer ordering dance. This time it almost worked. The waiter went to the back room and returned with four beers. They were at room temperature, which was 93 °F. As desperately thirsty as I was, a 93°F beer is not, well, a beer. My father instilled several universal truths in me early on and one had to do with the concept of an ice cold beer, preferably a Schlitz. When difficulties forced him into an early retirement, drinking and smoking wise, he confided that the only thing he really missed was a cold beer. He said, quite rightly, it is impossible to enjoy a ham and cheese on rye without a cold beer.

The Interpreter came to the rescue, ordering food and ice for the four of us. The large chunks of ice were disturbingly the same size and shape of the rocks on the last stretch of road. They were also peppered with what looked like the smaller stones on the road. This didn't bother the Driver and Interpreter at all, who chopped them with a pick, put the pieces in the glass, and poured the beer over the "ice". Nick and I recoiled at the prospect of getting cholera, preferring instead to construct a jury-rigged ice containment device to cool down the beer cans from the outside. Now we had to wait an eternity—5 minutes—for the beers to cool down to an acceptable temperature.

This wait gave Nick and me time to reflect on how outrageously frustrating it is to try to have a satisfying alcohol experience in Vietnam, or most of Asia for that matter. With all the things they do so well, you'd think they could get the booze thing right. You can get a spectacular eight-course meal in Vietnam for three dollars. And that's in a pretty good hotel. On the street you can eat that well for 50 cents. But try ordering a rum and Coke and you get nailed for $5 for a 7/8 ounce shot of rum (adoringly measured out like it's plutonium), plus $5 for the Coke, for a grand total of $10. If you want it on ice, well, you get looked at like you're a disease. Forget ordering a bottle of wine with dinner. You get some knock-off French vin ordinaire with a name like "Chateauneuf Too Pooped to Pop" for about $40. The only way to go, of course, is to order a local beer which is invariably tasty but invariably way, way too warm. The only place you can get cold, reasonably priced beer is at tourist bars in Hanoi or Ho Chi Minh City with names like "DMZ" or "Apocalypse Now" which, as you might imagine, I could never convince Nick to go into.

This conversation went on just long enough for our beers to cool down. I fired mine down in a microsecond, and then ordered another six-pack and a block of ice. The Driver appreciated this gesture very, very much.

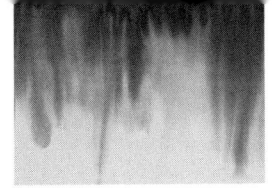

Hot Dogs

WHEN THE FOOD ARRIVED, NICK WONDERED how the four of us could possibly put a dent in the mountains of rice, rabe broccoli, onions, and "specialty meats" on the table. We suspected that they were curious to see how much I could actually polish off before I would end up majestically exploding as if we were playing out a Monty Python skit. When the Interpreter began to fill our bowls, I waved him off. I tried to explain that in spite of what might have seemed obvious concerning my appetite and eating habits, I actually rarely eat during the day. I followed this concept immediately by pointing to Nick's bowl, urging the Interpreter to give him my portion.

"What the hell do you think you're doing, Jim?" Nick was worried.

"Listen, Nick, you know I'm just smoking and drinking for lunch. But you better eat up or they'll be offended." Nick's sense of protocol really had him in a pickle now. He's not a particularly big eater anyway (except for pasta, in which case he could eat a swimming pool full), and I suspected that the kaleidoscope of emotions he had been experiencing, coupled with the fact that he hadn't eaten dog and chicken lips for almost three decades, started to turn his green eyes brown. But, as usual, he dug down deep inside, and began to wolf down both his, and my, portions.

While the three of them ate, I began to crank up the conversation. ~

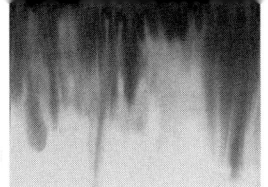

And Baby Makes Three

I KNEW WE WERE RUNNING OUT OF TIME AND I had to work fast, especially while Nick was forcing down endless portions of haute cuisine in the cafe.

"Okay, Nick, what was her name again?"

"Forget it, Jim. Let's just eat and leave. I'm satisfied."

"C'mon, Nick, just humor me—spell it."

"Jeezes, Jim. I don't know...H-'m-o-n, or H-u-m-a-n, or H-i-m-a-n or H-e-m-a-n . . . something like that."

"My vote's for Heman," I decided as if I knew the first thing about Rhade surnames. "Let's go with that one."

I motioned to the man and woman who owned this cafe. I found some paper and began to do something which at the time seemed perfectly natural to me. I wrote down the name "Heman" on a sheet of paper, pointed to the name and shrugged my shoulders with both arms held upward. To me this clearly meant, "My brother-in-law Nick and I are looking for a woman with the first name 'Heman'. Have you seen her hanging out lately?" To them it meant, "get me another six pack of beer," which they did. The Interpreter, and especially the Driver, hailed this second helping with a hearty toast to me.

Nick just looked at me and said, "Nice try, white boy."

I obviously had to elevate my communication skills up a notch. So I drew a picture. I must tell you that for a rank amateur, I'm pretty damn good with a pencil and sketch pad.

"Nick, I know you don't remember her last name, but what did her father do for a living?"

Nick paused, looked around, and whispered to me. "He was the Rhade tribal chief of this district."

Aha! This was going to be easy. I started to sketch. As the picture developed, I became aware of a gathering of townspeople standing around the table. I don't know what happened to me this day. I can easily hold a belly full of beer, or a fifth of Crown Royal without having my snappy conversation, or, for that matter, my ability to draw being adversely affected. In fact, I'm one of those lucky people that actually performs *better* on a couple of drinks. So it wasn't the beer. Whatever it was caused me to sketch the most primitive stick figure drawing I've ever made since kindergarten. The actual drawing I made that day is:

Below it I drew a simple, universally understood, proportionality statement that went:

$$\frac{\text{Heman}}{\text{Rhade}} = \frac{\text{Jim}}{\text{American}}$$

Which, of course, means, "Jim is to an American as Heman is to a Rhade." I was sure that the cafe owners, the Driver and Interpreter, and all the gathering crowd would understand this drawing and proportionality statement. I continued confidently. "You see, Heman is a Rhade, or maybe M'nong or H'mong, which sounds a bit like Heman, but assume she's Rhade". I was on a roll now. "Furthermore, this person Heman, who is now 55, was the daughter of a village chief and his wife, as shown in this clearly illustrated figure, as it would have appeared in 1967."

My expectations were less than fulfilled after two things happened. First, Nick asked, "What the hell is that supposed to mean?" This was immediately followed by the cafe owners and gathering crowd all gasping. As they recoiled collectively, I instinctively pointed at Nick. As usual, in tight or testy situations, he responded with one of his infinitely variegated poker faces.

"Well, you've really done it now, Jim." I knew I was on my own. He continued, "You've just told everyone here that I have returned and I won't be denied."

"Look at the drawing, Jim. There are only three possibilities. One—that I'm the King of New Jersey and I came back to find the child I sired in this town. Two—that I've got a dick that is s-o-o-o wonderful that all of the women here should want to have sex with me. Or three—that I'm here and I want to sleep with the Chief of this village."

I looked around at the faces of the townspeople as they stood there, mouth and eyes agape. The body language was unmistakable. Nick was right. That is exactly what I had proposed to the fine townspeople of Gia Nghia that sunny afternoon. Before I had a chance to dig myself a deeper hole, everyone scattered. One guy hopped on a motorcycle and tore out of town. I looked at the Interpreter, then Nick. They both jerked their heads to let me know that it was about time we headed back to Saigon.

So I ordered another round.

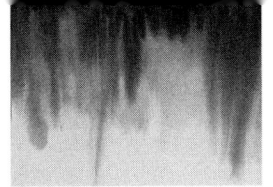

Ladies In The Shadows

WE WERE ALONE AGAIN IN THE CAFE. THE four of us just sat, quietly. This was unacceptable to me. I attempted to initiate a generic conversation about how the Vietnamese, and the Rhade, were gracious hosts to Americans, in spite of the havoc we had brought them. Their open friendliness was revealed clearly in this decidedly un-touristy town. They neither wanted nor expected anything from us. There were simply kind, open, and friendly, and we both agreed that the 21st century belonged to the Asians, and, goddamn it, they worked their asses off for it. It's a good thing that they have such a positive attitude about work, family, and visitors. Unless, of course, I had just poisoned the whole scene with that giant penis drawing I had conjured up.

Nick and I continued our one-minute monologues to each other while the Driver and Interpreter wolfed down their remaining buckets of rice. We were both very impressed with the whole notion of the Vietnamese not holding a grudge against Americans. According to my reasoning, it wasn't like the French and the Germans, who fight over actual real estate every fifty years or so when Germans get a burr under their saddle. Or the Jews and Muslims, who've also been able to convince the entire planet that we should all care about who's the king of the sand dunes. Or the Hutus and the Tutsis in Rwanda, who've reminded everyone that even blacks wage horrendous racial wars against each other. Or, in the ultimate bullshit war of all time, the Serbs and Croats, who have come up with some of the greatest non-reasons to butcher each other up.

We had been spared the non-ending cycle of vengeance with the Vietnamese. No land involved. No religion involved. No racial crap involved. But best of all, we didn't understand one thing these people were about. This makes for great friendship, under the right circumstances. To top it off, they seemed to be good capitalists. But although Americans had written and produced a ton of books and movies about the Vietnam War, we still haven't been able to resolve what happened. Especially the real soldiers. Like Nick.

After ten minutes of this conversation, I felt I was ready to make a really good speech to Nick, demonstrating once and for all, my profound insights on how group-think creates war. My speech was cut short by the glimpse of someone standing in the shadows of the cafe.

She had these beautiful, bright, smiling eyes that shone through the darkness of the room. As she walked forward out of the darkness toward our table, I looked at Nick, who glanced at her over his shoulder. She walked in slow steps toward us, then looked at Nick and gave him the most subtle smile I had ever seen. He didn't flinch.

She couldn't have been more than three years old, and her faint smile revealed one of the worst hare lips and cleft palates I could ever imagine. We were transfixed by this little girl, who seemed to pour out her entire heart and soul with her sad little smile. She turned and walked away into the back of the cafe. Nick sat, frozen. My eyes followed her. At that moment, I noticed another figure standing in the back of the cafe. She was in a darkened area, so I couldn't make out her face or features, only her outline. But I could tell she was looking at Nick.

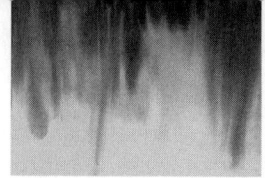

The Boss and His Secretary

I COULD SEE HER STANDING IN THE BACK OF THE cafe, but Nick had his back turned to her. Then the owner of the cafe motioned to me. Sensing that this might be show time, I picked up the Interpreter's translation book, some paper, and sauntered to the back of the cafe.

I walked right up to her. As her face became illuminated, I could see that she was a Rhade woman in her fifties. My pulse began to race.

"Heman?" I asked.

She just shook her head.

I was disappointed but she could be a key contact who came to the cafe to check us out. The motorcycle rider who had disappeared so quickly from the cafe stood behind her. I asked her to join us at the table but she wanted no part of being seen in the cafe. I sat down with her at a table in the rear of the cafe and I began one of my pantomime acts. Then I desperately flipped through the Interpreter's translator book, looking for any sky hook at all to help me communicate with her. Finally, I found lesson #56, which had the heading, "The Boss and His Secretary."

This was not, exactly, the relationship Nick and Heman had in 1967. Nick had mentioned, in fragmented bits and pieces, that she was the interpreter for him and his roommate. Heman would translate and adjudicate certain transactions for Nick in Gia Nghia and when they both went off into the jungle on patrol. She knew the jungle, mountains, and villages well, and she was an indispensable guide on where to go, and, most importantly, where not to go. Even more of her time was spent with Nick's roommate, an American army doctor. Heman would go out with him to the outlying villages to tend to the sick. This was America's main PR diplomacy to win the hearts of the villagers during the war. The Viet Cong played the same humanitarian game. At any rate, it was a bit misleading to use "The Boss and His Secretary" to explain Nick's relationship with Heman. But it was the best I could do under the circumstances.

So I pointed to the caption, then to Nick, and then to my sketch of the 'boner king' and his family, and then attempted to set the record straight. I feigned a hug, a kiss, and a bump and grind motion with my hips; then a no-no move with my index finger. Then I pointed to Nick and the picture again. This time, my intended message was, of course, "Nick and Heman weren't lovers. They just had an official Special Forces jungle relationship." The woman seemed to understand. At least it didn't cause any further gasps or looks of horror. Or maybe we were just ready to move on to the real story. I watched this woman's eyes carefully.

Finally, she said, "Heman . . . my friend." Hot damn, I thought, we have a live one! She then wrote a few words down for me. They were "1975—Heman—London." She put the pen down, smiled politely, shook my hand and walked away. Armed with this minimal, but significant, information, I started to walk back to the table. As I turned, the motorcycle guy grabbed my arm and motioned for me to come back to the woman. I walked forward and she leaned toward me. She whispered two letters in my ear. I was stunned, and I didn't know what to tell Nick next. ⁓

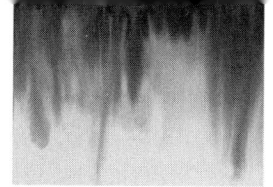

You've Changed

When I got back to our table Nick had already finished paying the check and the boys were up and ready to go.

"Time to go." Nick had seen enough and was ready to blow this particular popcicle stand.

"What's the rush?" I asked, knowing damn well that we really had to go.

We walked out to the car, got in, and the Interpreter waved good-bye.

"Whoa! Where are *you* going?" I asked him. He patted me on the arm and made some gestures that the Driver seemed to understand. Not that he had been a particularly essential part of our journey. I asked him for his reader, which he was happy to hand to me. We drove off, waving a combination of 'thanks', 'aloha', and 'nice' time to bail on us you bastard' hand gestures to the Interpreter. As we left I felt decidedly unfulfilled. Nick, sensing my disappointment, helped me out.

"Well, Jim, did you find anything out?"

"Yeah." I hesitated. "A bit of info. That woman is a

friend of Heman. She said Heman left in 1975."

"To?" Nick leaned toward me in the back seat, letting his knee touch my knee. I knew this meant he was becoming very focused on the issue at hand.

"London."

"London?"

"Yeah, London."

Nick's shoulders relaxed and he sighed quietly in relief. "Thank God she made it out." His entire body depressurized and sank into the back seat. He became as fully relaxed as I had ever seen him. I swear I even heard a sphincter unpucker a notch or two. Heman had made it out of Vietnam, safe and sound. This knowledge seemed to give Nick a heavenly moment of pure happiness.

Now, you see, I'm a scientist. My entire being—mind and heart—should always tend to choose truth over good feelings. But in a weak moment, I threw it all away. He seemed so at peace at that moment, I just couldn't finish the woman's message for him. ～

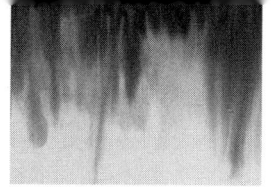

Sort Of On Our Way Home

LUNCH HAD REJUVENATED THE DRIVER. HE gunned through the first four gears of the Toyota with confidence. He left the market and the rest of the city center in a swirl of red dust. The lube job of a six pack of Dac Lac lager didn't hurt either. The first few turns he negotiated leaving town even had a certain flair to them. But I was celebrating our exit out of Gia Nghia prematurely.

At the edge of town the Driver turned off the road into a parking area in front of an establishment that is hard to describe in one word. It was a blend of machine shop, auto repair garage, one-table diner, and cattle crossing. Sort of a Hudsucker's sheet metal shop meets Anderson's Pea Soup in the Australian Outback. Whatever.

We got out of the car. The Driver motioned for us to go into the "diner" portion of the rest stop. He engaged one of the mechanics, pointing to several sections of the Toyota, which seemed to have the car equivalent of asthma, chest pains, and lumbago, in spite of the fact it was parked, motionless. We watched in mild disbelief as the Driver opened the trunk and took out the flat tire to be fixed. What the hell happened to parallel processing? Shouldn't he have been getting this tire and everything else fixed while we had lunch? Nick and I gave each other that Freemasonic look of mutual understanding that the Driver had blown it. Now we had to wait and waste time while they tended to the once youthful and dependable Toyota, which we knew would soon degenerate like the One-Horse-Shay. We'd never make it back to Saigon tonight. Or tomorrow night. This delay would cost us plenty of money and time and hassles and would screw-up the rest of our trip. Most importantly, I would not get to do the one thing I wanted to in Vietnam, because the Saigon Racetrack was only open on Sunday. The rest of my trip would be ruined. ⌒

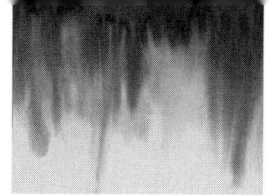

Play It Again, Nick

I SAT DOWN AT THE ONLY TABLE IN THE PLACE. There were only three short stools at the table. Nick, in a gesture of simple charity, offered all three of them to me. Nick walked outside to the dirt parking area in front of the establishment. I ordered a beer and bummed a smoke from a young woman, who was apparently assigned to take care of my needs for the duration of the tire changing. The afternoon sun was starting to make a bee line for the horizon. It was 3 p.m. and 88° F—the temperature of my beer. But by this time I was willing to suspend my high standards as I drank it at an ambient temperature.

I sat alone, staring out the glassless window. Out of nowhere, a soccer ball flew by. Then it whipped back again. I heard some kids laughing. Then I heard Nick laughing. I leaned outside the window to witness Nick playing a pick-up game of soccer with a couple of seven or eight year olds. They were way out of their league playing soccer with Nick. They would toe and heel the ball, then head it to Nick. Nick, true to his character, just caught the ball with his hands each time, then threw it back to them. The three of them played on and on, and the kids appeared to tolerate Nick's insistence on playing his version of the sport. They might have enjoyed it even more if he had been playing actual soccer.

The game was interrupted by the motorcycle guy.

This time I could see he had a passenger on the back of his machine. He broke off the main road into the parking lot at an unnecessarily high speed and steep angle. Apparently the word had spread all the way from Sa Pa that Evel Knievel was in the area, and to impress him, you'd better ride dangerously. He and a middle aged woman got off the motorcycle, walked past Nick and the kids, and stepped into the room where I sat. At this point the Interpreter, who we thought we saw the last of, came jogging down the road. After the motorcycle guy "introduced" me to the woman, the Interpreter entered the room and sat down at the table, not saying a word.

The woman was also Rhade and in her mid-fifties, and I began by using hand signals and body language to communicate. From what I could tell, she was the best friend of Heman—or Heman herself. I excused myself for a moment and leaned out the door.

I called to Nick, "There's someone in here you might be interested in meeting."

Nick came in, looked at the woman, then at me. "I think this might be your gal, Nick."

Nick gave me a screwy look, then started to speak to the woman.

"Heman, is it you?" he asked. She nodded yes. Nick moved forward, held out his hand, and continued. "How are you?—you look healthy." He paused. "I heard you were in London."

The woman just smiled.

Nick excused himself, then turned and murmured to me, "If this is Heman, then she's gained fifty pounds, forgotten how to speak English, and has shrunk two inches." Nick smiled at her and sat down.

I stood up and walked over to the woman with my pad and pencil. I kept out of earshot of the table, where Nick, the Interpreter, the Driver, the kids, the motorcycle guy, and a new forming crowd gathered.

I wrote down the name "Heman." She shook her head yes and said "friend." Okay, this was Heman's friend. I then asked "London?" She shook her head again. She then pointed to the town and said, "here, Heman."

Jackpot!

After going back and forth a few times the woman wrote down "Buon Mi Thuot—hopital." So that was it. Heman, who had worked so closely with Nick and his roommate the American doctor, had become a nurse and now worked in the hospital in the Dac Lac town of Buon Mi Thuot.

I excused myself for a moment, and told Nick the news. Nick bolted straight up from his chair and, in an unusually animated way, yelled "She's here? Heman is here? "

The woman nodded yes as Nick rocked, like he was a sprite with bells on his toes. I walked back to the woman. I wasn't finished with my questions.

I wrote down the two letters the woman in the other cafe had told me. I then wrote, "1975?" She shook her head no. She wrote down "1968" and nodded yes.

At this point the Interpreter became curiously serious and started to ask the woman something. They went back and forth in conversation for a few minutes. I looked up and noticed that the cafe was surrounded by fifteen or twenty people peering in through the open windows and the door. The mechanic, holding our tire, leaned through the door, listening intently.

Nick leaned over and asked me, "What is going on?"

At that moment the Interpreter turned to me. The look he gave me was unmistakable and dead serious. He nodded toward the door and said "Saigon—NOW." I knew at this moment it was time to leave. I motioned to Nick, who also got the Interpreter's message loud and clear. We stood up, shook the woman's hand, and walked out of the cafe. As we did, Nick couldn't take it any more.

"Jim, what the hell was going on in there?"

At this point I knew I had to tell him something I was sure would crush him. The woman he trusted, the only person he felt close enough to during the war to come back and see, had been a double agent.

"Viet Cong, Nick. Heman was Viet Cong ."

The Gathering Storm

I EXPECTED THE WORST. INSTEAD, NICK DIDN'T miss a beat. He just asked, "Yeah, but is she okay?" I nodded yes and he was ecstatic. To my utter amazement Nick couldn't care less about who she was or what she had become. All he cared for was her health and safety. At that moment I started to understand why he couldn't talk about the war. He really loved these people. And he cared profoundly for them, regardless of any political games. I wondered how many more servicemen like Nick there are out there. My guess is there are lots, only this is a side of the war I never heard about. But somehow I felt this circle hadn't quite been closed. There was probably more.

We walked out, then decided to have our picture taken with Heman's friend and the two kids Nick had been playing soccer with. She looked very relieved when she saw that Nick was still smiling, in spite of the otherwise bad news she had given us.

The Driver, Interpreter, and mechanic were putting on the finishing touches to the repairs on the Toyota. Basically, this involved wiring together the muffler and the rest of the exhaust system. Some leaks were also inspected but nothing could be done to stop the bleeding. The Toyota was dying and we all knew it. Could it get us back to Saigon? The Driver beckoned for us to move as a herd of water buffalo marched through the parking lot, surrounding the Toyota. When they cleared we hopped in, waved good-bye to the woman and the others, and drove away.

Not much was said as we negotiated our way back out of town. I felt our mission was sort of accomplished, and the prospect of spending the next seven or eight hours on the Road of Eternal Agony, was sobering.

I wish I could say the same for the Driver. The six pack had not worn off and he was driving like the proverbial bat out of hell. There was no pussyfooting of the sort he had done on our drive up to Gia Nghia. His attitude had clearly changed, and I wasn't convinced that the Toyota could tolerate the change.

Nick looked over and asked, "What time is our flight tomorrow?"

"Four thirty. Why?"

"We're never going to make it," he said in resignation

It was now 6 p.m. and the sun was about to do the slam-dunk drop it is so fond of at the equator. Sunset lasted only two minutes and we were rapidly sinking into total darkness. In the distance, the atmosphere glowed from a developing thunderstorm. Subtle flashes of crimson illuminated the rain that began to fall from the base of the clouds, but which never reaches the ground.

"Virga," I said.

"What do you mean, Jim?" asked Nick.

"Check out the virga at the base of those thunderheads. Up above the storm is raging, but the rain that starts to fall passes through some dry air, so the rain evaporates before it can reach the ground. It's called virga."

Nick was interested. He kept his eyes fixed on the virga.

It was a beautiful sight, but we certainly didn't need the help of rainstorms to lubricate Highway 14 for us.

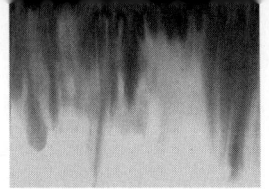

Rockets Red Glare...

WE RUMBLED DOWN THE ROAD IN RELATIVE silence. The silence was broken when we hit the border town and sped through a police checkpoint, slipping low into our back seat and shielding our faces with our hats.

We cleared the border check and the Driver took the Toyota down the fall line of what we knew was the most trying stretch of Highway 14. Unlike the drive up, on the drive down the Driver was fast and loose. And although he seemed completely reckless, which we blamed on the beer, he rarely hit a large rock or rut. A fair amount of the drive down he did with no lights on, using starlight and the lightning flashes in the southern sky to guide him. I was terrified.

Nick finally spoke. "What's gotten into him?," referring to how significantly improved his driving was now that it was dark, and he was drunk.

"Beats me," I said. "He seems completely transformed."

Nick nodded. The real question was, of course, had Nick been transformed? I was pretty much drained from the struggles of the day, while Nick seemed quite okay. The problem is, with introverts, you never really know what the hell's going on in their heads. That's why we extroverts never completely trust them. While we're wearing our hearts on our sleeves, they're holding back, watching, waiting—to say nothing of using our energies to suit their needs. I entertained the notion that Nick had planned to use my extroversion to his advantage for the entire trip. All the while he would feign reluctance in finding a way to Gia Nghia, and let me rudely press everyone for information on Heman's whereabouts. Plus he knows I can't control myself. That's it, I thought. He's been using me all along. Somehow, though, I didn't mind being used and I started to audibly laugh to myself, like someone who's lost their mind—having severed all important serious axonal connections in their brain due to a fourteen hour long auto accident.

"What's so funny," Nick asked.

"Nothing, Nick," I said, adding, "both funny bones snapped long ago."

The flashes of lightning were getting closer and I entertained the idea of having to negotiate the storms in the middle of the night on this road.

Nick looked out his open window, staring at the lightning flashes. His mood turned noticeably somber, and he retreated inside himself again. I didn't want him to drift off too far, since I still had some unanswered questions from some earlier conversations we had that day.

"Nick, remember that conversation we had this morning about what a wonderful little Catholic boy I was?"

"Yes," he replied.

"Well, I was trying to search my memory banks for something I was ashamed of, or something I did that I now regret." I pushed on. "Why did you ask me that question?"

"No particular reason," he said. "I was just curious."

We said nothing more for about twenty minutes.

I suspected he wanted to tell me something but I really didn't know what. I started to stab around in the dark a bit, but I was missing the mark.

Then, out of nowhere, Nick opened a small door and let me in.

"Jim, you've been asking me for a long time what it was like over here during the war."

I didn't flinch and he moved on.

"I'll tell you something that will surprise you. Most of us who served in Vietnam still think about it all the time, but we don't talk about it. We never did, not to our families, not to each other. We're all in our 50's now and we'll meet on a business trip, or at a party, and we'll discover in casual conversation that we served together in Vietnam. We feel an instant kinship, maybe spend the rest of the night milling around each other, but we don't talk about the war—especially those of us, like me, who were professional soldiers, not draftees. And do you know why, Jim? I know it sounds a little crazy, but we all, thirty years later, still feel personally responsible. Like if we had done our jobs better, or differently, we would have won that war. That's why we still take the war so personally; that's why we're so defensive about it, that's why we don't talk about it. We can't help feeling personally responsible for lying to the South Vietnamese, for leading them to believe that we would be their saviors. That if they just listened to us, believed in us, followed us, everything would turn out all right for their country. And we can't help feeling personally responsible for abandoning them in the end. Surely, the ones that helped us the most, that were the most courageous and loyal, suffered the most when we left. If we talked about those feelings of guilt, Jim, people would laugh at us, would tell us we're crazy, and that wouldn't make us feel any better. The fact is, Jim, we just didn't keep any of our promises to these poor people, and they suffered terribly because of it. We abandoned these people. We promised—I promised..."

He stopped his sentence to collect himself.

"We came here, we told them we'd stay with them to the end. We'd fight with them. We'd protect them, their families . . . their children. We broke that promise and I feel . . ."

He stopped again and looked out the window for a moment. He took a deep, sad breath and went on.

"I can't really explain the feelings I've had . . . anger . . . shame . . . guilt . . . betrayal . . . personal loss."

Nick was in freefall. ～

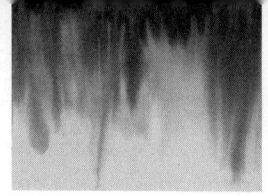

The Bombs Bursting In Air . . .

NICK SANK INTO HIS SEAT, BUT SHOWED NO outward signs of distress. He was one tough hombre and I knew he had gotten it under control. But I still had nothing to add to this conversation. He was on his own, but he switched gears on me again.

"There's something I haven't told you yet," he said.

"What's that?"

"My roommate . . . " He paused and went on. "Heman and my roommate, the doctor, spent a lot of time together, walking from village to village. You know, treating pneumonia, cholera, malaria . . . " He continued. "Heman fell in love with him. The whole year she fell deeper and deeper in love. She wanted to marry him, move back to the states with him."

"What happened?" I asked.

"He never returned it. They were as close as a man and woman could ever get. But as far as I know, they never had sex. And he left early, in 1968, leaving her behind."

Nick and I now knew what had happened. In the insane maelstrom of politics and war something significant had happened in Gia Nghia. A young Rhade woman, the only daughter of an important tribal chief, risked her life as an anti-communist freedom fighter, and she fell madly in love with a young American doctor. Together, they brought babies into the world, saved lives, and eased the burden of these people. When he left, he left her alone. Her whole world turned upside down and in late 1967 or at the beginning of the Tet offensive in 1968, love, politics, and war blurred together into an unimaginable crazy quilt of emotions. So, she turned Viet Cong. And that was that.

"I do remember, now, just one more thing," he added. "Whenever Heman and I would walk to the villages, she always walked close by, urging me to go this way . . . never that way." Nick knew then that Heman was in tight with everyone, and she had protected his ass every step of the way.

I suppose some of us are lucky enough to have an angel looking over us. Nick certainly had his and now he knew how difficult the whole scene must have been for her. I didn't know where to go from here, or how to get closure. So I asked an obvious question.

"What would have happened to you if you had walked down the wrong path?"

Nick pondered my question carefully, deliberately, and it took him about ten minutes to begin an answer.

"Someone did, Jim . . . someone did."

I waited. "Who was it, Nick?"

"One afternoon, my roommate and I were relaxing after lunch in our room. Heman ran up, knocking and yelling at us through the door. We ran out, following her to the triage. When we walked in, the room was filled with an unmistakable smell."

"What was it," I asked.

Nick paused, then went on. "Phosphorus . . . Heman ran to a bed and my roommate and I ran after her. On the bed was a boy, about twelve years old. His face and body were covered with burns. He had picked up one of our unexploded phosphorus grenades on a trail. He pulled the pin, and it went off in his face."

Nick sagged and took a breath.

"For the next two hours we watched the boy bleed from the burns in his lungs. He finally choked to death. It was the worst thing I ever experienced in my life."

He tried to continue.

"It's one of those things in my life . . . " Nick missed the next beat and choked on his next words . . . "that I regret the most ."

This moment crushed him. And me, too.

I don't know why Nick took such personal blame for the death of that young boy. Maybe someone in his unit dropped the grenade. Maybe he dropped it. But probably not. Whatever happened, he didn't deserve this. But Nick seemed to take full responsibility for that boy's death. And for thirty years he had suffered in silence.

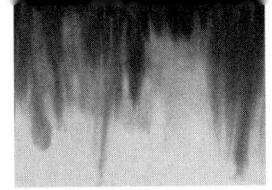

The Last Supper, The Last Smile

TWENTY MINUTES HAD PASSED, OR AT LEAST it seemed that way. Actually two and one-half hours had passed. Then we had a rude jolt, as the Toyota launched off the dirt and on to the paved part of Highway 14, an hour and a half northeast of Saigon. The road was smooth but the silence was truly deafening. We had almost made it.

The last flat would happen at 2 a.m., just three miles from our hotel in downtown Saigon. The flat would be met with wonderment and a toast from Nick, the Driver, the Interpreter, and me, as all of us were in awe of the Toyota, a true underdog which had beaten The Road.

The Toyota and the Driver had turned, quite to our bewilderment, into a finely tuned team. The Driver was blind and utterly inept when the sun was out, when he was well-rested, and was sober. But turn out the lights, fill him up with a six pack, and make him drive all day and night, and the guy was a marvel.

The Interpreter had seemed to be as useful as tits on a bull, up until the moment of truth when his eyes clearly communicated when we really had to get out of Gia Nghia.

But I hadn't understood how this guy from the Mekong Delta seemed to know so much about the remote parts and people of Dac Lac.

The grueling trip was nearly over, but the Interpreter and Driver wanted to stop one more time, since they were hungry and thirsty again, and wouldn't get home to the Delta until 5 a.m. or later. The Driver pulled into a somewhat upscale open air cafe in the next town. We got out, ordered some food, and sat at a table outside, near the road. It was midnight, but people of every age were walking about, enjoying the relative coolness of the late evening.

We ate and drank and congratulated each other for still being in one piece. I then pulled out some of the pieces of paper I had used that afternoon in Gia Nghia to try to communicate with everyone. Nick had a good laugh at my drawing one more time, and then I noticed that the Interpreter was staring intently at the piece of paper on which I had written "Viet Cong," and "1967, 1968" and "1975." He put his fork down and stopped eating. Sensing something was wrong with him, I pointed to the letters "V.C." and intimated the question "Were you V.C.?"

Nick interrupted my efforts and said, "Jim, don't you realize that by 1975 we had lost the war and everyone was V.C?"

But the Interpreter didn't look at Nick. He just looked me straight in the eye, held his hand up high in the air, made a fist, and slammed his fist into this thigh.

I was confused. Then he repeated the action, each time with a more serious look. I was still in the dark. The Interpreter then picked up his reader, leafed through the pages, and located the words.

He said "V.C . . . killed my father . . . in Gia Nghia."

At that moment I realized the pain the Interpreter had gone through that day, returning to Gia Ngha, perhaps by accident, with a former American soldier, to re-live some awful memories of his own. It was a very depressing moment watching him have to explain himself to us. But after that, he seemed to be in much better spirits. Perhaps he, too, had undergone an exorcism that day. He just lifted his glass of beer, said 'cheers' to all of us, and then went on eating. We finished, paid the bill, and drove away.

We drove out of town, turned south on the direct route to Saigon, and eased on down the paved road.

After a half hour or so, I turned to Nick, who was wide awake. I had one more question for him, and I hoped it wouldn't be the one that pressed him too far.

"How does this all end, Nick?"

"Jim, I think you know."

We were both thinking the same thought.

"I think the main problem would be convincing her parents to fly to the states to have the surgeries done," Nick said. "Money and transportation are no problem at all."

"Maybe we could get the chopper ride in and out of Gia Nghia after all." I was chomping at the bit now.

"When we get back from our trip, I've got some people who would love to help us out," I added.

But Nick knew the potential problems much better than I did. The Vietnamese officials might balk at him helping a young Rhade girl with a hare lip and cleft palate. Why not use the resources for an ethnic Vietnamese child? The Rhade have great pride in the singular decision making imperatives of the family, especially the clan leader. Would he go along with it? We tried to think of all the problems and obstacles to what we both wanted to do.

But whatever obstacles there were, I was sure Nick would find a way to make it work, and to make the entire family whole again. Especially the little girl with the beautiful eyes in Gia Nghia. And, hopefully, she would soon have a smile to match those eyes. ～

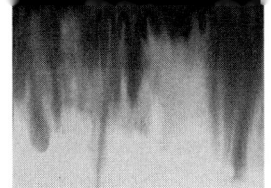

Long Shots

WHEN I RETURNED HOME FROM THE TRIP, my friends, and especially my family, noticed a difference in me. They said I had become an incoherent idiot. I had begun to rattle on about how our lives are blessed with Drivers who are blind, Interpreters who are mute, inadequate modes of transportation with poor clearance and tortured roads to nowhere. My inability to communicate anything of substance about my trip with Nick to anyone else had become utterly frustrating. It got so bad that my brother told me I was beginning to act like one of those Vietnam Vets who came home from the war and couldn't speak to anyone.

I was able to tell him that we did get to Saigon racetrack on Sunday and although I couldn't get the hang of the highly cryptic Vietnamese racing form, I did learn how the Vietnamese felt about their horses.

Nick and I were successful in buying our way into the Jockey Club, which meant one desperately important thing—we were able to buy ice cold beer. We also had the pleasure of meeting one other American there. He was an

IBM executive who wore a Rolex on one wrist and a local chick on the other. He was miserable living in Ho Chi Minh City and it was clear that the only pleasures in his tour of duty were on Sundays when he was able to bet the ponies and bird-dog the honeys at the racetrack. He seemed to think it was a fair deal.

Although the quality of horses, or more accurately, flea bitten little nags, was abysmal when compared to our usual stock and trade at Del Mar and Santa Anita, the thrill of the races still gave me pleasure that day. I must confess I didn't win one race—not even close. What made it particularly tough is there was no win, place or show betting. Just quinellas, which meant that in order to win, both of your horses have to come in one-two. Not easy. But in between races I did get to watch Nick. As he jabbered on and on with the IBM operative about business opportunities and life in Saigon, I just watched and listened.

I do have a notion on how we communicate with each other. We use the left side of our brain to speak the literal, syntactic, grammatically correct truth of our thoughts. We use the right side to put rhythm and heart into our words. But I've never really understood where the soul of language comes from. Until Nick showed me the way. Through his years of silence he had been singing loud and clear. I just wish my ears had been tuned a bit better.

In the dissolve of that spring afternoon at the Saigon racetrack, I groped for meaning. All I came up with were losing quinella tickets. I wanted to stay to the bitter end, until I lost everything or lit up the scoreboard with a winner, any winner. But Nick, the practical son of a bitch that he is, tore me away from the track, and said we had to leave soon so we could make our flight to Jakarta. When he said that, I realized what I hadn't heard the entire day of Saturday's ride to Gia Nghia. He finally belted out a hearty snort, and his patented, "HMM . . . HMM-HMM-HMM."

I waited long enough to see my last horse lose. That scrawny plug of a pony, who couldn't have been more than ten hands high at the shoulder, was led off the track by his young trainer, who must have been only twelve years old. The pony had run the worst race I had ever seen in my life, and he was huffing and wheezing in the torrid heat of the equatorial sun.

When this loser had been led far off the track to the privacy of the back stable area, I watched the trainer stop and face the pony. He grabbed the pony by the ears and appeared to sternly chastise him for his poor performance. I winced. Then the young boy leaned forward and gently kissed the pony on the muzzle. As the pony bobbed his head up and down and flicked his tail, I knew I was watching a winner. It turned out to be the best day I ever had at the track, by a long shot. ～

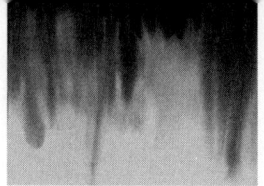

The Final Ascent

THE FINAL LEG OF OUR TRIP WOULD SWEEP US through Indonesia, land of thirteen thousand islands and 200 million people. Freed from the burden of a set schedule we would ultimately aim for some mindless hedonism in Bali. We devoted nearly three full hours to fully enjoying Jakarta, so that we could round out our meager photo album. More snapshots of Nick standing at attention in front of various and sundry banks and financial institutions in the capital city.

We then set off to the airport to fly to Yogajakarta to visit the Buddhist temple, a true wonder of the modern world. At the airport we were disappointed to learn that the flight was full, having been chartered by a horde of junior high school kids from the States. This did not deter us. Faced with this mild stroke of negative serendipity, we sought out another destination, using the criterion of choosing a place with the most unpronounceable name. We found it—Ujung Pandang—the regional big town of Sulawesi and historical home of the infamous bogeyman. Once in Ujung Pandang we learned of a most extraordinary people, the Torajans, who were located in the remote Central Highlands of Sulawesi. We sweated out a semi-scheduled flight on a two-engine eggbeater to the mountain village of the Torajan people.

In the States we spend much of our family wealth on our daughters' weddings. In Mexico, families spend it on their daughters' coming-out parties, and the Jews have perfected the art of lavish partying on their childrens' Bar Mitzvahs. The Torajans have created a different angle on spending all their money. They throw a funeral party you just wouldn't believe.

After witnessing one of these amazing spectacles, Nick and I found a guide to lead us to their burial grounds, in the limestone cliffs in the surrounding mountains. Families are interred in caves cut into the cliffs and mounds of skulls and bones are heaped in piles below these burial vaults. High in the cliffs, life-like wooden statues of the dead stand on ledges carved into the cliffs. The beautifully crafted figures facing the villages below ultimately disintegrate into dust as the years go by. The scene, as hauntingly complete as it seemed, had something missing. There were no wooden figurines of any babies, some of whom must have died in these families. We pointed this out to the guide, who just told us to follow him into the jungle.

We walked on a narrow path through a forest of giant bamboo. Finally we came to the edge of a small clearing. In the center of the clearing stood an enormous tree, with a broad trunk that reached high above the bamboo forest. The guide pointed to the top of the tree's canopy. Set in the highest branches was a huge eagle's nest which looked as old as the tree itself. Then we looked down at the trunk. Our jaws dropped.

Cut into the trunk were thirty or so rectangular holes, about the size of a small child. The holes were covered by the darkened fibers of a coconut husk. This matting was nailed into the trunk by wooden pegs. In between these recently cut chambers were slits and scars in the trunk. Nick and I just stood next to each other, awestruck.

Our guide then told us that the Torajans say that when a baby dies, they are not really dead. Their bodies are buried in the tree, which produces copious amounts of sap. The sap, like a mother's milk, is said to nurture the child in preparation for its actual death, which occurs when the bark of the tree grows over the entrance of the living tomb. This process takes twenty or thirty years, when the small scar in the bark closes up. When the scar finally heals, the eagle leaves the nest, bringing the soul of the child to heaven.

Our guide's story was cut short.

At that moment the eagle at the top of the tree came out of his nest and circled the tree, slowly lifting itself to the sky above.

The healing of the spirit takes time, and only when it is ready can we let go. Our last flight out of bondage can be painful, but it is always beautiful.

Nick and I were ready to go home.

AFTERWORD

When Nick returned later that year to Vietnam, I didn't go with him. He would ultimately find Heman and together they would help to make a small Rhade girl with a harelip and cleft palate whole again. I did not ask Nick what he and Heman did or talked about. That's their business. Maybe some day when we're too old to travel and act like cool guys he'll tell me something, in some way, that I'll understand.

Those of us who are safely tucked away at home will never understand the terror and nightmare of war. But all the warriors leave a trace, a camouflaged signpost to lead us to their story, if we care to look. They may be crying on the inside, but those virga tears must dry up as they pass through that emotional arid territory, in their soul, and we never see those tears.

When I returned home from our trip, my family was able to find out after forty years what happened to my uncle following his own personal hell in Iwo Jima.

One week before he died in 1974, my uncle told a young man a story, one that tore at my uncle for years.

The Japanese soldier he saved on that brutal island in 1944 did not fare well after the war. My uncle sought out the soldier for twenty years and finally found him in Japan. He decided to bring him to America, where he lived secretly in a small room in a barn on my uncle's farm. They both knew the stigma and retribution that would occur if any of their friends found out they lived together, side by side, transcending the endless prejudices that war brings. They, too, had found their way home.

Jim Fallon is a professor of Anatomy and Neurobiology at the University of California, at Irvine. He has written over a hundred and fifty research articles and books on the structure of the brain, and spent a year in Kenya in 1990 on a Fulbright Scholarship. He has been a Sloan Scholar, as well as the recipient of numerous teaching awards, and has also appeared in neuroscience features on CBS, NBC, ABC, PBS, and the Discovery Channel.

He lives in Irvine, California with his wife. The father of three adult children, he is an avid fisherman, downhill skier, gourmet cook, wine connoisseur, screenwriter, scrabble player, and horse handicapper. He has traveled extensively to over fifty countries throughout the world.

To order this and other Dickens Press titles,
Please call or write:

DICKENS PRESS
P.O. BOX 4289
IRVINE, CA 92616
(800) 230-8158
(949) 725-0788
FAX (949) 856-3201
dickenspub5@yahoo.com
www.geocities.com/dickenspub5

Individuals: To order Virga Tears, send $12.95, plus $2.00 shipping, add $1.00 for each additional book. Enclose money order, check, Visa or Mastercard number.